CALL to CELEBRATE EUCHARIST

Author

Maureen A. Kelly, MA

Program Consultants

Mary Birmingham

Rita Ferrone

Gael Gensler, OSF

Mary Ann Getty-Sullivan

Rev. Joe Kempf

Tom Kendzia

Rev. Paul Turner

Reviewers

David Haas

Rev. Robert J. Hater, Ph.D.

Contributing Artist

Michael O'Neill McGrath, OSFS

Harcourt Religion Publishers

www.harcourtreligion.com

Nihil Obstat
Msgr. Louis R. Piermarini
Imprimatur
✠ Most Rev. Robert J. McManus, S.T.D.
Bishop of Worcester
August 9, 2005

The Imprimatur is an official declaration that a book or pamphlet is free of docrinal or moral error. No implication is contained therein that anyone who granted the Imprimatur agrees with the contents, opinions, or statements expressed.

For permission to reprint copyrighted material, grateful acknowledgment is made to the following sources:

Division of Christian Education of the National Council of the Churches of Christ in the U.S.A.: Scripture quotations from the *New Revised Standard Version Bible*. Text copyright © 1989 by the Division of Christian Education of the National Council of the Churches of Christ in the U.S.A.

GIA Publications, Inc., 7404 S. Mason Ave., Chicago, IL 60638 www.giamusic.com 800-442-1358: Lyrics from "Send Us Your Spirit" by David Haas. Lyrics © 1981, 1982, 1987 by GIA Publications, Inc.

International Commission on English in the Liturgy: From the English translation of the *General Instruction of the Roman Missal*. Translation © 2002 by International Committee on English in the Liturgy, Inc. From the English translation of and original alternative opening prayers from *The Roman Missal*. Translation © 1973 by International Committee on English in the Liturgy, Inc.

International Consultation on English Texts: English translation of the Nicene Creed and the Lord's Prayer by the International Consultation on English Texts (ICET).

United States Catholic Conference, Inc., Washington, D.C.: From the English translation of the *Catechism of the Catholic Church* for the United States of America. Translation © 1994 by United States Catholic Conference, Inc. — Libreria Editrice Vaticana. From the English translation of the *Catechism of the Catholic Church: Modifications from the Editio Typica*. Translation copyright © 1997 by United States Catholic Conference, Inc. — Libreria Editrice Vaticana.

Photo Credits
Bettmann/Corbis 30; "From the Housetops" Publications 70; *San Pascual Bailón adorando la Eucaristía*/reprinted courtesy of Museo de Bellas Artes de Valencia 60.

Illustration Credits
Dan Brown/Artworks 36–37; Shane Marsh/Linden Artists, Ltd. 6–7, 56–57; Roger Payne/Linden Artists, Ltd. 26–27; Francis Phillips/Linden Artists, Ltd. 76–77; Clive Spong/Linden Artists, Ltd. 16–17, 46–47, 66–67.

Printed in the United States of America

ISBN: 0-15-901640-1

1 2 3 4 5 6 7 8 9 10 153 10 09 08 07 06 05

Contents

Philosophy and Process iv

Components and Web Site v

Scope and Sequence .... vi–vii

Catechetical Communities viii

Restored Order ix

Sacraments and Liturgical Catechesis .... x–xi

The Role of Music xii

Respecting Cultures .... xiii–xiv

Welcome xv

Children's Lessons

Chapter **1** We Belong 2A

For Restored Order implementation, use these two sessions after Chapter 1:

Restored Order (Confirmation): Gifts of the Spirit CE23–33

Restored Order (Confirmation): We Are Holy CE34–44

Chapter **2** We Gather 12A

Chapter **3** We Are Forgiven 22A

Chapter **4** We Listen 32A

Chapter **5** We Prepare 42A

Chapter **6** We Remember and Give Thanks 52A

Chapter **7** We Share a Meal 62A

Chapter **8** We Go Forth 72A

Catholic Source Book

Words of Faith 82–87

Order of the Mass 88–99

Receiving Communion 100–101

Catholic Prayers 102–105

Index 106

Program Resources, Activity Masters, and Scripture Stories

We Belong CE1–2

Restored Order (Confirmation): Gifts of the Spirit CE23–33

Restored Order (Confirmation): We Are Holy CE34–44

We Gather CE3–5

We Are Forgiven CE6–8

We Listen CE9–10

We Prepare CE11–12

We Remember and Give Thanks CE13–15

We Share a Meal CE16–19

We Go Forth CE20–22

Philosophy

Call to Celebrate: Eucharist flows from the traditional Church teachings that:

- Liturgy, the public worship of the Church, is the central activity of the People of God.
- The Eucharist is where the faithful come together to offer praise and thanks, and to celebrate God's presence and promise.
- In the celebration of the Eucharist, the People of God are transformed by their immersion in symbols, rituals, prayers, and participation in the Body and Blood of Jesus Christ.
- Participation in the Eucharist urges the faithful to apostolic witness and action for justice in the world.

Call to Celebrate: Eucharist upholds the principle that preparing children for participation in the Eucharist through the reception of First Communion is a two-part process. First, it is a process of initiation that is best done in the midst of family, peers, and the whole community. Second, it is a process of liturgical catechesis that respects how individuals—both children and adults—come to know the mysteries of faith through participation in symbol and ritual.

Catechetical Process

At its heart, *Call to Celebrate: Eucharist* follows a liturgical-catechetical method in three steps:

CELEBRATE

Every session begins with a celebration that includes a ritual focus. These celebrations involve children, families, or whole communities in a gradual unfolding of the rites, symbols, and prayers of the Eucharist. The celebration is immediately followed by a reflection on what was experienced.

REMEMBER

In every session, a scripture passage that pertains to the Eucharist is proclaimed and broken open. The doctrines that form the body of teaching about the Eucharist are presented and a specific part of the Eucharistic ritual (or Mass) is explained.

LIVE

Every session includes an activity that helps children integrate the theme into daily living.

Activity Strand Every session is developed around an activity strand:

- Reflect
- Share
- Respond

Our Catholic Teachings...

The goal of liturgical catechesis is to prepare people for and initiate them into the mystery of Jesus Christ and in the full, conscious, and active participation in the Liturgy. It is through catechesis that we understand the nature, rites, and symbols of our faith.

See *Constitution on the Sacred Liturgy*, 10; *National Directory for Catechesis*, 33; John Paul II, *Catechesi Tradendae*, 23; and *Catechism of the Catholic Church*, 1075.

Child's Book helps children reflect on the mystery of the Eucharist through celebrations, colorful and appealing visuals, and interactive pages with activities and prayers. Faith at Home features and pages help families support children in their preparation.

Catechist Edition provides everything the catechist needs to be successful—easy-to-use planners, theological, spiritual, and historical background, an easy-to-use three-step lesson process, a wealth of resources and activities, plus activity masters and scripture pantomimes, dramas, and narrations.

Family Guide features reflections for all adult family members who are preparing children and also offers step-by-step outlines for families preparing children in the home.

Songs of Celebration CD offers the songs used in the celebrations for *Call to Celebrate: Eucharist*. It may be used in the catechetical sessions and by families.

My Mass Book is a delightfully illustrated guidebook for children that presents the Order of the Mass.

Stories of Celebration presents dialogue with children, parents, and noted catechists and liturgists to help parents and catechists reflect and understand their role in preparing children for First Communion and to understand the meaning of the Eucharist.

Certificates are full-color mementoes that you may personalize for each child once the first Sacrament of the Eucharist has been celebrated. Each certificate provides a space for the pastor to sign and the church seal to be affixed so families have an official record of the celebration to take home and frame if desired.

Sacraments Source Book provides a wealth of information and practical resources, including professional development articles, catechist and parent orientation and training sessions, family centered sessions, and parish assembly sessions.

GO ONLINE www.harcourtreligion.com

This site provides more background and activities for children, parents, and catechists.

- Print Planner with Links
- Music Sample
- Illustrated Glossary
- Timeline of Jesus' Life
- Catechist Edition Activity Masters
- Catechist Edition Gospels
- FAQs
- Extended Saint Stories
- Symbol Chart

People of Faith: Generations Learning Together Celebrating the Sacraments: Eucharist magazine, Vol. 4, issue 3, engages all ages in a series of faith-filled articles and activities about the Eucharist.

Scope and Sequence

	Chapter 1 WE BELONG	Restored Order: Use these sessions if also preparing for Confirmation. GIFTS OF THE SPIRIT	WE ARE HOLY	Chapter 2 WE GATHER	Chapter 3 WE ARE FORGIVEN
Ritual Focus	Renewal of Baptismal Promises	Blessing	Extension of Hands in Blessing	Procession and Gloria	Penitential Rite
Scripture	The Vine and the Branches John 15:1–17	Jesus Promises the Holy Spirit John 14:15–26	Jesus Teaches about Holiness Luke 4:16–30	The Early Christians Acts 2:42–47	The Call of Matthew Matthew 9:9–13
Faith Focus	• A sacrament is a holy sign that comes from Jesus and gives us grace. • Baptism, Confirmation, and Eucharist are Sacraments of Initiation. • The Sacraments of Initiation make us full members of the Church.	• The Holy Spirit is the third Person of the Holy Trinity. • The Holy Spirit is our Advocate, our helper. • We receive the seven gifts of the Holy Spirit at Confirmation.	• The gifts of the Holy Spirit help us do God's work. • The Holy Spirit makes us holy. • Being *holy* means "being close to God and choosing what God wants."	• The Church is the People of God and Body of Christ. • The Eucharist, or Mass, is the Church's most important action of praise and thanks. • The Introductory Rites gather us as a community of faith.	• The Eucharist is a sacrament of unity and forgiveness. • Sin keeps us from being one People of God. • At Mass we ask God's forgiveness during the Penitential Rite.
Catechism of the Catholic Church	1212, 1275–1277, 1285, 1316–1317, 1321–1327	1830–1831	1302–1305	1153, 1156–1158	1393–1395
Liturgical Focus	Sacraments of Initiation	Bishop's Laying on of Hands, Prayer for the Gifts of the Holy Spirit	Anointing, Final Blessing	Introductory Rites, Gloria	Penitential Rite
Signs of Faith	water Paschal candle Holy Trinity	extending hands chrism bishop	fire miter and crozier saint	assembly procession prayer and singing	Lord Have Mercy silence sprinkling with holy water

Chapter 4 WE LISTEN	Chapter 5 WE PREPARE	Chapter 6 WE REMEMBER & GIVE THANKS	Chapter 7 WE SHARE A MEAL	Chapter 8 WE GO FORTH
Signing	Honoring the Cross	Memorial Acclamation	Sharing a Meal	Blessing for Mission
The Sower Matthew 13:1–23	The Washing of the Feet John 13:1–16	The Last Supper Matthew 26:26–28; Luke 22:14–20	I Am the Bread of Life John 6:30–58	Pentecost Acts 2:1–41
• The Bible is God's word written in human words. • We listen to the word of God during the Liturgy of the Word. • When we listen to God's word, we want to share it with others.	• Jesus sacrificed his life for us when he died on the cross. • The Mass is a sacrifice. • At Mass through the power of the Holy Spirit and the words and actions of the priest, Jesus offers again the gift of himself to his Father.	• The Eucharistic Prayer is a prayer of thanksgiving, remembering, and consecration. • Through the power of the Holy Spirit and the words and actions of the priest, the bread and wine become the Body and Blood of Jesus. • At the Great Amen, the assembly says "yes" to all of God's saving actions and promises.	• The Mass is a meal of thanksgiving. • Jesus is the Bread of Life. • In Holy Communion, we are united to Jesus and the Church. We share in the promise of life forever with God.	• The Eucharist changes us. • The Holy Spirit helps us to live out our mission. • At Mass we are sent forth to love and serve others.
101–104, 136, 141, 1154, 1190, 1349, 1408	1333–1336	1362–1366	1382–1398	1391–1397
Liturgy of the Word	Preparation of the Altar and Gifts	Eucharistic Prayer, Consecration, Memorial Acclamation, Great Amen	Communion Rite	Dismissal
Sign of the Cross Bible readings	cross altar bread and wine	kneeling priest Blessed Sacrament	Sign of Peace paten, ciborium, and chalice Lamb of God	blessing witness deacon

Catechetical Communities

Family

The primary place where catechesis occurs is in the family. It is within the family that children first learn about God. The family is where they continue to develop values, practice their faith, and observe and witness to a faithful life lived in common everyday experiences.

In *Call to Celebrate: Eucharist*, "family" encompasses all those people who make up the basic unit of a child's primary community: parents, siblings, and extended family members. *Call to Celebrate: Eucharist* involves the family through:

- Faith at Home activities and pages in the *Child's Book*
- A *Family Guide*
- Parent sessions in the *Sacraments Source Book*

Catechist

Your role as a catechist for children's sacrament preparation is significant. As a person of faith, your witness and sharing of faith is vital. You create the environment for celebrating and learning. Through you, children will come to know the mystery of God's love in the Eucharist in a unique way. In your role as catechist for *Call to Celebrate: Eucharist,* you are called upon to preside, proclaim the word, listen, reflect, and teach. Your ministry is a gift to each child because through your efforts children will come to a deeper appreciation of the Eucharist and the signs, symbols, and rituals associated with it. They will also be led to a fuller experience of Jesus and the Church.

Assembly

The participation of the worshiping community is important to children's initiation. The vitality and faith life of the assembly shapes and forms the faith of its children. The *Sacraments Source Book* provides blessings, general intercessions, and bulletin notices to alert the assembly to remember and pray for the children as they prepare for their full initiation. It also provides assembly gatherings in which members of the assembly and families can engage together to reflect on the rites and their meaning. This program encourages the *full, active, and conscious* participation of the whole community. Remind children and their families of the importance of participating with the assembly every week in the Eucharistic celebration.

Restored Order

In the early Church, Christian Initiation was one event. Adults or children were baptized, anointed, or had hands laid upon them, and then participated in the Eucharist, all at the same celebration. For a variety of reasons this practice gradually became separated into three different events. In 1910, Pius X recommended in his encyclical *Quam Singulari* that the First Communion of children should not be deferred too long after they had reached the age of reason. Previous to his urging, children who had been baptized as infants usually celebrated First Communion in the early teen years, and Confirmation usually was celebrated at an earlier age. However, once children began to participate fully in the Eucharist at an earlier age, the age for Confirmation was varied and not necessarily tied to reception of First Communion.

As a result of Rites issued by the Church after the Second Vatican Council, many dioceses and parishes throughout the United States have adopted the practice of celebrating Confirmation prior to First Communion. This is often referred to as *restored order*.

Some of these dioceses celebrate the Sacrament of Confirmation at the same Eucharistic celebration in which children celebrate their First Communion. Other dioceses celebrate at a different time, but before First Communion.

Other dioceses choose to celebrate Confirmation sometime after First Communion. All of these practices are approved by the United States Bishops Conference, which has given approval to the celebration of Confirmation for children baptized as infants anytime between the ages of seven and sixteen.

Call to Celebrate: Eucharist includes two sessions for those parishes that are practicing restored order. These sessions are found on pages CE23–44 of this *Catechist Edition*. If you are preparing children for both sacraments, you would use these sessions after session one.

Our Catholic Teachings...

There is a great deal of variation from diocese to diocese for the age of confirmation in the United States. The Sacrament of Confirmation can be celebrated at any time between the age of discretion and sixteen years. It has been determined that a single catechesis cannot be assigned for this sacrament.

See *National Directory for Catechesis,* 36 A, 2.

SACRAMENTS AND
LITURGICAL CATECHESIS

Liturgical Catechesis

There is an ancient Latin phrase which is still used today that reinforces the importance of liturgical experience for an authentic appropriation of Christian faith. It is *lex orandi legem credendidi statuit,* which means, "the rule of prayer establishes the rule of faith." Liturgical catechesis is the activity of bringing communal faith to consciousness through participation in and celebration of the rites of the community. It has a solid historical tradition in our Church since liturgy has long been regarded as the Church's "school of faith," an expression which recognizes the formative value of ritual celebration on participants. The story of Emmaus shows that it is precisely in the ritual "breaking of the bread" that the disciples come to know and understand the mystery of Jesus (Luke 24:13–35).

Children

Liturgical catechesis meets a child's readiness to learn. Research shows that children are impressed most deeply in the context of rituals and symbols. They are capable of entering into them and able to express profound insight into the meanings expressed in religious symbol and ritual. Participation in religious ritual and symbol landscapes their imaginations and provides formative experiences that go beyond the written or spoken word. In *Call to Celebrate: Eucharist,* children are gradually led through celebration with symbol, ritual, and gesture to understand the mystery of the Eucharist in an age-appropriate way. Every session of *Call to Celebrate: Eucharist* begins with a celebration that is an essential part of the lesson. These celebrations help children better understand and enter into the liturgical life of the Church. Taking their cue from the *General Directory for Masses with Children*, "…the Liturgy itself always exerts its own inherent power to instruct" (12); the celebrations are meant to be the cornerstone on which each session is built.

Prayer Space

Therefore, it is very important for you to take care to prepare the prayer space ahead of time and to lead the celebration in a way that will call children to prayer, participation in the ritual action, and reflection after the celebration.

The prayer space needs to be a place where the movement of processions and rituals are easily and reverently participated in. Prepare it ahead of time. You may choose to set aside a space in your meeting place, or you may find the church or another room to be more suitable. When you have chosen a space, arrange it in such a way

Our Catholic Teachings...

Parish catechetical programs that provide catechesis on the Mass are an essential tool in preparing children for their first celebration of the Sacrament of the Eucharist. It is through these programs that children learn how to participate fully, actively, and consciously in the Mass.

See *National Directory for Catechesis*, 36, 3a.

that children can move easily and can see and hear everything that is happening. Decorate the space with plants or flowers. Always have available a large clear bowl with holy water, a Bible and stand, and a candle. Check your planning page each week to be sure you have everything you need for the celebration.

The Celebration

Each of the celebrations is built around a song, a scripture reading, and a ritual action. With the exception of Chapter 3, all of the celebrations also include a procession. Take time to conduct the procession reverently and slowly. Involve children in song, either by leading it yourself, using the *Songs of Celebration* CD, or inviting a song leader into your group. You may choose to proclaim the Scripture from the adapted version in the *Child's Book* or from the Bible. Be sure to familiarize yourself with the ritual action ahead of time so that you are able to be fully engaged with the children during the celebration. The celebration is in the *Child's Book*; if you find that having children use the books during the celebration is distracting, you may wish to do the celebration without them and guide the children's responses.

Leader of Prayer

During the celebration you are the leader of prayer. The way you preside is important. Here are some tips:

- Learn the script ahead of time. Be familiar with it, so that you are able to lead and be present with the children without being distracted or fumbling for "what comes next."

- Use your body to communicate. Stand tall. Use broad and expansive gestures. Be aware of your facial expressions and tone of voice.

- Watch your timing. Let there be silence between parts of the prayer. Take time with each child during the ritual actions. Do not be afraid of pauses or silence. They often lead children to deeper prayer and reflection.

Reflection

Liturgical catechesis does not end with the celebration. It is important to allow children the opportunity to reflect on the celebration and to articulate what they have experienced. During this segment of the session, it is more important that you listen to the children's responses and take your lead from them than for you to tell them what it means.

THE ROLE OF MUSIC

Regardless of age, ethnic origins, or belief systems, it is difficult to imagine anyone who would reject the life-giving power of music for children and adults. Music taps into feelings and at times provides a sense of the transcendent. Songs can tell a story and they can be a textbook. Music and song that touch our lives and are related to significant experiences often come back over the years and tap into our memories and imaginations.

These same things can be said of the music used in liturgy in general and in the celebrations of *Call to Celebrate: Eucharist* in particular. In incorporating music into the celebrations of *Call to Celebrate: Eucharist,* keep in mind that the music provided is an integral part of the celebration and learning experience of the children. It is an important catechetical element, since music forms, shapes, and gives voice to what we believe, truly "echoing" God's word and action in our lives.

The program includes a *Songs of Celebration* music CD to use in the celebrations. Alternative suggestions are also given in each session. If you are not confident in your musical abilities, do not let your lack of musical skill lead you to abandon music as part of the content. Use the CD or engage a musician to help you and the children experience the fullness of the celebration and closing prayer. You can also use the music throughout the lesson as background while the children are working on activities.

Song Titles for *Songs of Celebration*

Yes Lord, I Believe! © 2000 John Burland

Glory to God, Marty Haugen © GIA Publications

Create in Me © Tom Kendzia. Published by OCP

Open My Eyes © Jesse Manibusan. Published by OCP

We Praise You © Damean. Published by OCP

Te alabaré, Señor/I Will Praise You, Lord/Tony Alonso
   © GIA Publications

We Come to the Table © 2004 John Burland

Lead Us to the Water © Tom Kendzia. Published by OCP

RESPECTING CULTURES

The Catholic Church is, by its very name and nature, universal. The Eucharist is a primary celebration of the Church's universality, but it is also a celebration that recognizes and draws forth the unique cultural contributions of people throughout the world. The *Catechism of the Catholic Church* states that the "mystery of Christ is so unfathomably rich that it cannot be exhausted by its expression in any single liturgical tradition" (1201) and the "celebration of the liturgy, therefore, should correspond to the genius and culture of the different peoples" (1204).

Universality of the Church

One of the elements of preparing children for the Eucharist must be to give them a sense of this universal dimension of the Church. Not only are the children going to receive the Body and Blood of Christ, but they are also entering into a new relationship with the Body of Christ, the Church, which is comprised of diverse cultures.

The catechist has a two-fold responsibility. The first is to incorporate an understanding of the universality of the Church in sacramental preparation, and the second is to ensure that she or he is aware of the diversity of cultures that may be present among children preparing for the sacrament.

Tips for Respecting Culture

The richness of our faith invites diverse cultures to celebrate a life with Christ. This concept can be tangibly expressed to children through the use of multicultural symbols and objects that celebrate the diversity of God's people. Use the following tips to help children learn that people around the world profess their faith in a variety of ways, and we are all children of God and beloved by him.

Chapter 1 Christ, the Light of the World, represents the fullness of life to all people. Give each child a white paper plate to create a mandala, an ancient symbol of wholeness through all cultures. Discuss what symbols children in other countries might use to show Jesus as the Light of the World.

Chapter 2 Catholics around the world gather to celebrate the Eucharist. The reality of what we believe about the Eucharist never changes, but the songs, languages, instruments, and actions used are sometimes different depending on the country in which the Eucharist is celebrated. Do one or more of the following activities:

- Listen to sacred music in another language.
- If a child in the class speaks another language, invite him or her to say the "Lord's Prayer" in that language.
- Practice bowing from the waist to each other as a Sign of Peace as many Asian cultures do.

Our Catholic Teachings...

The multicultural and pluralistic society of the United States poses unique opportunities and challenges for the faith. Through the inculturation of the Gospel message, faith and life are linked, and the faithful can receive Jesus in every aspect of their lives.

See *National Directory for Catechesis*, 21C.

Chapter 3 The Eucharist reminds us that we are all part of God's family. Write new lyrics to the tune of "He's Got the Whole World in His Hands," using the names of countries and children throughout the world.

Chapter 4 After reading the Parable of the Sower and the Seed, tell the children that Jesus wants each of them to be like the rich soil, so the seed of his love will grow in them and make the world a better place. Have the children create a chain of good deeds with construction paper and place the chain around a globe. Place the globe in a prominent place.

Chapter 5 The altar is called the table of the Lord and all are welcome to gather around it. For the closing prayer, cover the prayer table with a multicultural cloth or cloth map (available at fabric stores) and place items on the table that represent different cultures. Gather children around the prayer table, explain the significance of the items, and ask the children to close their eyes and think of what the world would be like if everyone lived in peace.

Chapter 6 The Eucharist joins our prayers with people the world over. Everywhere people raise their voices and thank God for his many gifts and blessings. Teach the children to say "thank-you" in a variety of languages.

Chapter 7 Jesus is the Bread of Life and invites us to take and eat the bread which becomes his body. To help children understand this concept, explain to them that people all over the world are nourished by bread. Bring in a variety of different types of bread for children to see and share.

Chapter 8 We are sent forth at the end of Mass to love and serve the Lord. Invite children to picture people all over the world leaving Mass ready to love and serve the Lord and prepared to live in peace. Ask children what the world would be like if everyone really cared about others.

CALL to CELEBRATE

EUCHARIST

Children's Lessons

Welcome

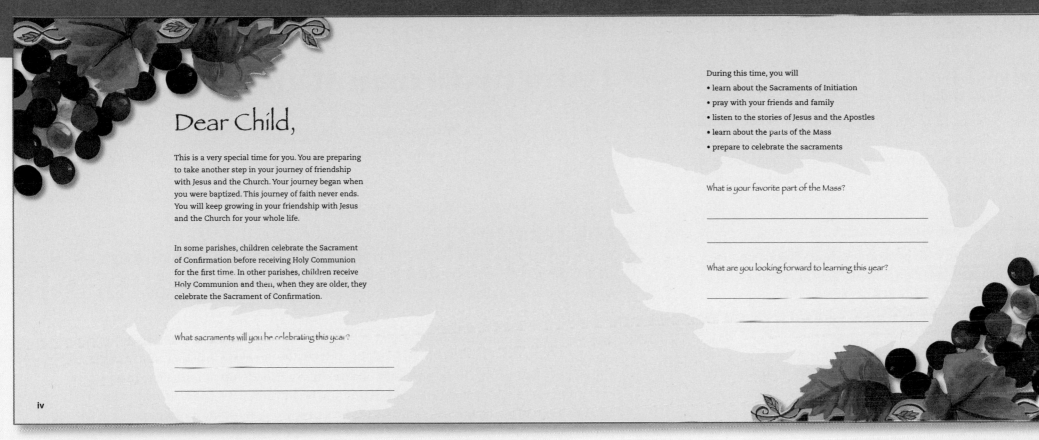

Dear Child,

This is a very special time for you. You are preparing to take another step in your journey of friendship with Jesus and the Church. Your journey began when you were baptized. This journey of faith never ends. You will keep growing in your friendship with Jesus and the Church for your whole life.

In some parishes, children celebrate the Sacrament of Confirmation before receiving Holy Communion for the first time. In other parishes, children receive Holy Communion and then, when they are older, they celebrate the Sacrament of Confirmation.

What sacraments will you be celebrating this year?

_____

_____

During this time, you will
• learn about the Sacraments of Initiation
• pray with your friends and family
• listen to the stories of Jesus and the Apostles
• learn about the parts of the Mass
• prepare to celebrate the sacraments

What is your favorite part of the Mass?

_____

_____

What are you looking forward to learning this year?

_____

_____

These pages provide a welcome to the program and the process of preparation.

Dear Child

▶ Read aloud the first paragraph.

▶ Discuss ways children can continue their friendship with Jesus, such as praying, going to Mass, and being kind to others.

▶ Emphasize that when we receive Jesus in Holy Communion, he is very close to us, and going to Communion strengthens our friendship with him.

▶ Summarize the second paragraph.

▶ If your group will be celebrating Confirmation before First Communion or has already celebrated it, spend some time talking about what will or did happen.

▶ Note that all children receive the Sacrament of Reconciliation before First Communion.

❓ Have children write their answers in the book. Help them with spelling. Reconciliation, Eucharist, Confirmation

▶ Ask volunteers to read the bulleted text on page v.

▶ Walk children through the book and show them examples of prayer activities, stories of Jesus, and parts of the Mass.

❓ Have children write their responses to the first question. Encourage volunteers to share their responses and the reason they chose that part.

❓ Read aloud the second question and write children's responses on the board or on chart paper. Have children go over the list and choose what they want to write in their books.

My Faith Journey (pages vi and vii)

These pages in the *Child's Book* are meant to be filled in as the children complete the process.

Encourage children to take their books home and have a family member help them complete them at the appropriate time.

Chapter 1

We Belong

General Instruction of the Roman Missal

"In the celebration of Mass, the faithful form a holy people, a people whom God has made his own, a royal priesthood,... Thus, they are to shun any appearance of individualism or division, keeping before their eyes that they have only one Father in heaven..." (no. 95)

Catechism Connection

To deepen your own background and reflection on the Sacraments of Initiation, refer to the *Catechism of the Catholic Church, 1212, 1275–1277, 1285, 1316–1317, 1321–1327.*

Catechist Resources

 The Church Speaks About Sacraments with Children
Mark Searle, Commentator
Liturgical Press
A collection of liturgical and catechetical documents that gives insight into the meaning of the sacrament

 Pope John Paul II's New Encyclical on the Eucharist
Lorene Healy Duquin
Our Sunday Visitor
Condenses the major points of the Church's teachings and makes an ideal introduction to the Church's teaching on the Eucharist.

Children's Resources

 Who Is the Spirit? *(14 min)*
Gaynell Cronin
St. Anthony Messenger Press
Shows the Holy Spirit as friend, helper, and teacher

 God Speaks to Us in Water Stories*
Mary Ann Getty-Sullivan
Liturgical Press
Shows how God connects with humans through the symbolism of water

 * *Available at* **www.harcourtreligion.com**

Catechist Formation

> "You are my friends if you do what I command you."
>
> John 15:14

A Friendship of Faith

Airport terminals are frequently the scene of touching and happy reunions. Family and friends who have been separated for a period of time greet one another and feel a strong sense of belonging. Baptized persons share a similar sense of belonging with one another because they are united in Christ.

The Sacraments of Initiation—Baptism, Confirmation, and Eucharist—join us as members of the Body of Christ. In these sacraments we receive Christ and he receives us. Christians share with Christ, and with one another, a friendship of faith. The profession of faith made at Baptism expresses the common bond Christians share as members of Christ's Body. The deep love of the Father, Son, and Holy Spirit becomes part of the life of Christians when they are baptized in the name of the Trinity.

Sacraments of Initiation

As members of the Catholic family, we are never alone. We belong to Christ and his Church. At Baptism, we receive the Light of Christ to remind us that we are to be a light to the world as Christ is. The gifts of the Holy Spirit are strengthened in us at Confirmation. We are sealed, anointed, and marked as totally belonging to Christ. We are strengthened to show the love of Christ to the world and to send a message that all are invited to belong to God's family. In the Eucharist, we share the Body and Blood of Christ and celebrate this communion of belonging and friendship that helps us grow stronger as a family.

When you think of Jesus as a friend, what qualities come to mind?

Why is being part of a faith community important to you?

Catechist Prayer

God, our Father, draw me into the circle of love that you share with your Son and the Holy Spirit; help me express and celebrate that love with others. Amen.

Lesson Planner

		OBJECTIVES	LESSON PROCESS	ACTIVITIES	MATERIALS
CELEBRATE	15 minutes Pages 2–3	**Ritual Focus** *Renewal of Baptismal Promises* To experience a celebration of the word, including the Renewal of Baptismal Promises	Celebrate the opening prayer.		**PROGRAM RESOURCES** *Songs of Celebration* CD, track 7 **OTHER MATERIALS** Bible, prayer table, candle, large glass bowl filled with water
	Pages 4–5	To explore the meaning of the ritual action To explain that through Baptism, we belong to God and the Church forever	Reflect on the celebration. Complete the activity. ✝ Read about and discuss water. Describe the Church as the Body of Christ, and discuss original sin, Baptism, and the Holy Spirit. Talk about what it means to be a Christian. ✝ Read about the Paschal candle.	**Reflect** Children reflect on the experience of the celebration and the meaning of renewing Baptismal Promises.	
REMEMBER	30 minutes Pages 6–7	**Faith Focus** *What does Jesus tell us about belonging to God?* To understand what it means to belong to God	Discuss belonging. 📖 Proclaim the Gospel story. *John 15:1–17* Complete the activity.	**Share** Children draw pictures of how they belong to God. **Faith at Home** Suggested activities for the home	**PROGRAM RESOURCES** Copies of Activity Master 1, p. CE1 Copies of Echo Pantomime 1, p. CE2
	Pages 8–9	**Faith Focus** *Which sacraments are signs of belonging?* To describe the Sacraments of Initiation	Identify the Sacraments of Initiation. Explain the terms sacraments, chrism, Baptism, Confirmation, Eucharist, Holy Communion. ✝ Read about and discuss the Holy Trinity.	**Faith at Home** Suggested activities for the home	
LIVE	15 minutes Page 10	To help children express that they are followers of Christ	Introduce the activity. Pray the Closing Blessing. Read aloud the People of Faith story about Blessed Carlos Manuel Rodríguez.	**Respond** Children complete a banner describing followers of Jesus.	**PROGRAM RESOURCES** *Songs of Celebration* CD, track 7
FAITH AT HOME	Page 11	**Faith at Home** To introduce the different parts of the Faith at Home page	Review the Faith at Home page. Encourage children to share this page at home.	**Act** Suggested activities for the home	**PROGRAM RESOURCES** Family Guide, pp. 16–17

CELEBRATE

Objective

To experience a celebration of the word, including the Renewal of Baptismal Promises

Preparation

Familiarize yourself with the movements of the ritual focus for the Renewal of Baptismal Promises on pages 2–3. You will need:

- a Bible
- a table covered with a white cloth
- a candle and a large glass bowl filled with water on the prayer table
- Use the *Songs of Celebration* CD, track 7, to rehearse the suggested song, "Yes Lord, I Believe!" or one of the optional music suggestions on page 3.

Select a child to carry the Bible in procession.

We Gather

Invite children to assemble with their books.

Gather children into the prayer space with a procession.

- Direct children to follow you and the child carrying the Bible, as you lead the procession.
- As you process, lead children in singing using the *Songs of Celebration* CD, track 7.
- When all are assembled, light the prayer candle.
- Begin prayer, and lead children in the Sign of the Cross.

CELEBRATE

Ritual Focus: Renewal of Baptismal Promises

We Gather

Procession

As you sing, walk forward slowly. Follow the person carrying the Bible.

🎵 Sing together.

I believe in God the Father
I believe in God the Son
I believe in the Spirit
And the strength that makes us one.

© 2000 John Burland

Leader: Let us pray.
Make the Sign of the Cross together.

Leader: On the day of your Baptism, your family and the Church claimed you for Christ.

You received the gifts of faith and new life. Today let us remember the promises of Baptism together.

Come forward, and gather around the water and candle.

Leader: Do you say "no" to sin, so that you can live always as God's children?

All: I do.

Leader: Do you believe in God, the Father almighty?

All: I do.

Leader: Do you believe in Jesus Christ, his only Son, our Lord?

All: I do.

2

✦ Liturgical Background

Baptismal Promises Three questions make up the profession of faith in the Sacrament of Baptism and the Renewal of Baptismal Promises. The questions are derived from the three sections of the Apostles' Creed, which had its beginnings in the ancient baptismal liturgy. The questions for the profession of faith express our faith in the Father, Son, and Holy Spirit.

We consider this profession of faith to be a promise. It commits us to something in the future.

When the profession of faith is made in Baptism, it implies that with God's help we will continue to believe and live according to the faith we have professed. The baptismal rite includes a rejection of sin before the profession of faith. The threefold rejection of sin parallels the threefold profession of faith.

Yes, I believe

Leader: Do you believe in the Holy Spirit, the holy catholic Church, the communion of saints?

All: I do.

Leader: This is our faith. This is the faith of the Church. We are proud to profess it in Christ Jesus.

All: Amen.

BASED ON RITE OF BAPTISM FOR CHILDREN 144–146

Leader: Let us come to the water and thank God for the gift of our Baptism.

One at a time, make the Sign of the Cross with the water.

[Name], you are the light of Christ.

Child: Amen.

We Listen

Leader: God, our Father, open our hearts to the Holy Spirit as we remember our Baptism. We ask this through Jesus Christ our Lord.

All: Amen.

Leader: A reading from the holy Gospel according to John.

All: Glory to you, Lord.

Leader: Read John 15:1–17.

The Gospel of the Lord.

All: Praise to you, Lord Jesus Christ.

Sit silently.

We Go Forth

Leader: Loving God, we thank you for the gift of Baptism. Send us forth to bring your love to others. We ask this through Jesus Christ our Lord.

All: Amen.

 Sing the opening song together.

3

Ritual Focus: Renewal of Baptismal Promises

• Follow the order of prayer on pages 2–3.

We Listen

For the proclamation of the Gospel, you may use a Bible or the adapted reading in the *Child's Book* on pages 6–7.

We Go Forth

Lead the closing prayer. As children process back to their seats, have them sing *Songs of Celebration* CD, track 7, "Yes Lord, I Believe!" or one of the optional music suggestions.

Optional Music Suggestions:

"Pan de vida," © Jaime Cortez. Published by OCP

"Taste and See," James Moore © GIA Publications

Ritual Background

Blessing with holy water Catholics bless themselves with holy water when they enter and leave a church. The purpose of this gesture is to recall their identity as baptized Christians. The Sign of the Cross and the blessed water are a reminder that every baptized person is solemnly signed with the cross and claimed for Christ in the rites of Christian Initiation.

Water is the central symbol of the Sacrament of Baptism. It signifies

• cleansing

• rebirth

• life

• God's grace

Every time we touch the blessed water, it is an opportunity to remember the mystery of God's life within us.

Objective

To explore the meaning of the ritual action of Renewal of Baptismal Promises

To explain that through Baptism, we belong to God and the Church forever

Liturgical Catechesis

The purpose of this section is to help children reflect on their experiences of the signs, rituals, prayers, and gestures of the celebration and to lead them to express their own meaning of the experiences. Allow children to share their experiences without commenting on them.

New Life

- On the board or on chart paper, write the following questions: What did you see? What did you hear? What did you do?

- Guide children to reflect on the celebration by reviewing what happened in the prayer.

- Encourage children to share their responses to the questions.

- Invite children to share stories or details they know about their own Baptism.

Reflect

- Ask children to write their responses in the book. Tell children they do not have to complete all three choices.

Water

- Read aloud the text.

- Invite children to make the Sign of the Cross with the water provided during the prayer celebration.

New Life

Water

Water gives life. It cleans and makes things like new. Water also reminds us of new life. The water used at Baptism is blessed. The blessed water is a sign that God the Father gives us his life and cleanses us from all sin. Through the waters of Baptism, we have new life with Jesus. Every time we go into a church, we bless ourselves with holy water. We remember our Baptism.

4

Reflect

Renewal of Promises Think and write about the celebration.

When I said, "I do"

_____

_____

When I put my hand in water

_____

_____

When I heard the words "the light of Christ"

_____

_____

Additional Activity

Make a mural   Place a large sheet or sheets of paper in a location (such as on the floor, the wall, or tables) where children can gather in a group or groups to draw.

- Discuss the many ways water and light help us in our daily life.

- Distribute crayons or markers.

- Invite children to draw one way that water or light helps them.

When the mural is complete, help children connect the meanings expressed in the mural to the symbols of water and light in Baptism.

The Body of Christ

Baptism makes us children of God and members of the Church, the **Body of Christ**. At Baptism, we are given new life with Jesus Christ. **Original sin** and all personal sins are forgiven. We receive the light of Christ and become his followers. People who follow Jesus are called disciples. Another name for a follower of Christ is *Christian*.

Through our Baptism, we belong to the Church and become special friends of God. We need Baptism to have life with God forever.

In Baptism, God the Holy Spirit comes to live in us. The Holy Spirit

- helps us believe and have faith
- shows us how to pray
- guides us to be the light of Christ for others and makes us holy
- helps us follow God's law

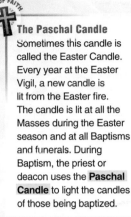

SIGNS OF FAITH

The Paschal Candle

Sometimes this candle is called the Easter Candle. Every year at the Easter Vigil, a new candle is lit from the Easter fire. The candle is lit at all the Masses during the Easter season and at all Baptisms and funerals. During Baptism, the priest or deacon uses the **Paschal Candle** to light the candles of those being baptized.

5

Teaching Tip

Preview the book Capitalize on children's interest in their new book to help them become enthusiastic about studying the Eucharist.

- Allow time for children to browse through the book.

- Point out that each chapter contains prayers, stories about Jesus, and information about the Eucharist.

- Remind children that all of you will work together on the book.

- Show children the Faith at Home page, and encourage them to get their family members involved.

- Allow a brief time for questions about the book.

- Show that you are happy to share this special time with them and their families.

The Body of Christ

Summarize the first two paragraphs for children. Emphasize that:

- Baptism makes us children of God and members of the Church
- another term for *Church* is *Body of Christ*
- Baptism takes away all sin

Ask children to read silently the last two sentences in the first paragraph and find two names for followers of Jesus. disciples, Christians

Read the third paragraph aloud to children. Invite children to stand and make these gestures with you for each statement about the Holy Spirit:

- helps us believe (Raise arms and hands to the sky.)
- shows us how to pray (Bow head and fold hands.)
- guides us (Place hand over eyes as if looking for something.)
- helps us follow God's law (Fold arms over chest.)

The Paschal Candle

- Invite several children to read the text aloud.
- Turn to page 86 in the illustrated glossary, and show children the picture of the Paschal candle.

Objective

To understand what it means to belong to God

Faith Focus

What does Jesus tell us about belonging to God?
List children's responses on the board or on chart paper.

We Belong to God

- Read the first paragraph aloud. Point out that Jesus had many friends while he was on earth. We can be his friends, too.

- Point out the illustration of the vine and the branches. Have children trace the connection between the vine and a branch with their fingers.

 Scripture   JOHN 15:1–17

The Vine and the Branches

- Gather children into a story circle or in the prayer space. Remind them that they will be hearing the story from the Gospel of John again.

- Ask what they remember from hearing the Gospel during the celebration.

- Or, tell the story using the Echo Pantomime 1 on page CE2 of this edition.

REMEMBER

We Belong to God

Faith Focus

What does Jesus tell us about belonging to God?

Jesus knew he would be returning to God, his Father. Jesus' disciples were sad. They wanted to stay close to him. Jesus wanted to tell his friends that he would always be with them. He wanted them to know that they belonged to him in a special way. So, he told them this story.

JOHN 15:1–17

The Vine and the Branches

"I am the true vine, and my Father is the vine grower. He takes away every branch in me that does not bear fruit. Every branch that does bear fruit, he cuts back so it will grow more fruit. A branch cannot bear fruit on its own. It must remain on the vine. You are the branches of the vine. As long as you stay close to me, you will keep bearing fruit."

6

📖 Scripture Background

The Gospel of John   The Gospel according to John does not have the kinds of story parables that are in the Gospels of Matthew, Mark, and Luke. Instead, images such as the vine and branches serve a similar purpose as the parables do in the other Gospels. In John, Jesus begins this speech with the words, "I am," identifying himself with images familiar to his disciples.

Elsewhere in the Gospel of John, Jesus says, "I am the bread of life," "I am the way and the truth and the life," and "I am the good shepherd."

The images are used to make a point and to challenge the listener to think beyond the ordinary.

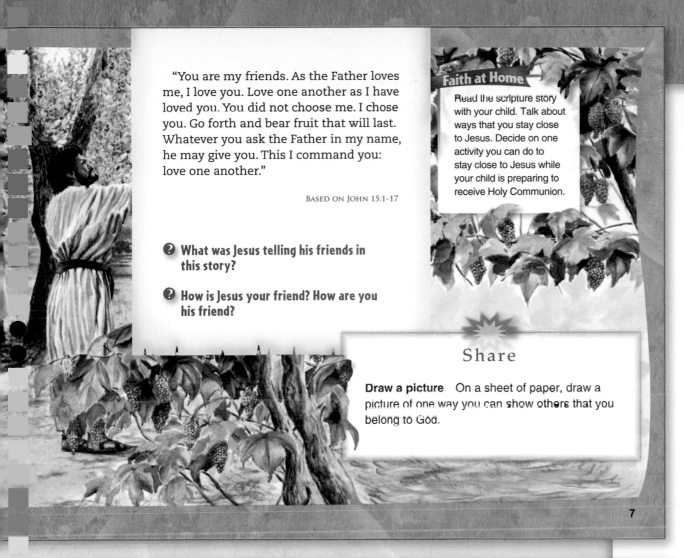

"You are my friends. As the Father loves me, I love you. Love one another as I have loved you. You did not choose me. I chose you. Go forth and bear fruit that will last. Whatever you ask the Father in my name, he may give you. This I command you: love one another."

BASED ON JOHN 15:1–17

Faith at Home

Read the scripture story with your child. Talk about ways that you stay close to Jesus. Decide on one activity you can do to stay close to Jesus while your child is preparing to receive Holy Communion.

❷ **What was Jesus telling his friends in this story?**

❷ **How is Jesus your friend? How are you his friend?**

Share

Draw a picture On a sheet of paper, draw a picture of one way you can show others that you belong to God.

7

---

❷ Invite children to share their responses to the first question. Accept all reasonable responses.

- Emphasize that Jesus wants us to know we belong to him, and he wants us to love one another.

❷ Ask the second question, and list children's responses on the board or on chart paper.

- Invite children to choose one way they will be Jesus' friend this week.

Share

- Read the activity directions aloud. Explore with children ways of showing we belong to God.

- Walk among children, and observe their work.

- Have volunteers share their completed pictures with the group.

Activity Master

You may wish to use Activity Master 1 on page CE1 to further integrate the meaning of the Gospel story.

▲ Activity Master 1

Review

- We belong to God.

- Jesus commands us to love one another.

Cultural Background

Farewell addresses The reading about the vine and the branches is part of a longer speech in John (John 14–17) sometimes described as the "Farewell Address." It was customary in Jewish tradition that at the time of his impending death, a father or leader would summon his heirs or disciples to review his legacy to them. In these farewell addresses, the speaker charges his heirs or disciples to carry on his life's mission and warns them of the dangers they will face in his absence. He cautions them to be faithful.

There are several examples of this tradition in the Scriptures. In the Old Testament, references are found for Jacob (Genesis 49), Moses (most of the Book of Deuteronomy), and Joshua (Joshua 24). In the New Testament, Jesus (John 13–17) is pictured as speaking about his death and what the disciples can expect after he is gone.

Objective

To describe the Sacraments of Initiation

Faith Focus

Which sacraments are signs of belonging?
List children's responses on the board or on chart paper.

The Sacraments of Initiation

Remind children that they begin their prayers with the Sign of the Cross, which names each Person of the Trinity.

- Summarize the information in the first paragraph.

- Write the terms *sacrament* and *Sacraments of Initiation* on the board or on chart paper. Use the text to explain what these words mean.

- Ask children to read the paragraph to find out how many Sacraments of Initiation there are. three

Baptism

- Point out the photograph of the child being baptized.

- Have children share what they recall about Baptisms they have attended.

- Read the text aloud.

The Holy Trinity

- Read aloud the text.

- Review the roles of each Person of the Holy Trinity.

- Have children make the Sign of the Cross slowly while naming each Person of the Holy Trinity.

The Sacraments of Initiation

The Holy Trinity

God the Father, God the Son, and God the Holy Spirit are the three Persons in one God. We call them the Holy Trinity. The three Persons act together in all they do, but each Person also has a special role. We sometimes call God the Father the Creator because he made everything. Jesus Christ is the Son of God and our Savior. God the Holy Spirit makes us holy. Each Person of the Trinity is called God.

Faith Focus

Which sacraments are signs of belonging?

A **sacrament** is a holy sign that comes from Jesus. Sacraments give us grace, a share in God's life. Baptism, Confirmation, and Eucharist are called **Sacraments of Initiation**. We are joined closely to Christ through these sacraments. They make us full members of the Catholic Church. They are signs that we belong to God and to the Church.

Baptism

In Baptism the priest or deacon pours water over our head or lowers us into the water three times. He says, "I baptize you in the name of the Father, and of the Son, and of the Holy Spirit." Then he rubs blessed oil on our head. This is called anointing. We need to be baptized only one time.

As a sign of our new life in Christ, we receive a white garment. Then the priest or deacon gives our parent or godparent a lighted candle. He prays that we will walk as children of the light and follow Jesus' example.

8

✦ Catechist Background

Sacraments   A sacrament is an outward sign of an invisible reality—that is, something we cannot see. The invisible reality of a sacrament is God's presence and action. Here are important things to know about sacraments:

- Sacraments give grace, a sharing in God's own life and friendship.

- The sacraments are actions of God and the Church.

- God the Father, God the Son, and God the Holy Spirit are always at work in the sacraments.

- There are seven sacraments: three Sacraments of Initiation (Baptism, Confirmation, and Eucharist); two Sacraments of Healing (Reconciliation and Anointing); and two Sacraments at the Service of Communion (Holy Orders and Matrimony).

Confirmation

The Sacrament of **Confirmation** strengthens God's life in us. Confirmation completes our Baptism and helps us grow as followers of Jesus. During Confirmation, the bishop or priest puts his hand out and prays:

"Send your Holy Spirit upon them
to be their Helper and Guide."

Then the bishop or priest lays his hand on our heads and anoints us with the holy oil of **chrism**. Oil is a sign of strength. He says:

"Be sealed with the Gift of the Holy Spirit."

These words tell us that we receive the Holy Spirit in a special way at Confirmation. Both Baptism and Confirmation mark us with a special character that shows we belong to Jesus.

Eucharist

The Sacrament of the **Eucharist** joins us to Jesus in a special way. The Eucharist is a sacred meal of thanksgiving. Jesus shares his own Body and Blood with us in Holy Communion.

You participate in the Eucharist by coming to Mass with your family.

❷ **How are the Sacraments of Initiation signs of belonging?**

Sacrament Background

Initiation and Conversion The process of initiation and the celebration of the Sacraments of Initiation have undergone a process of change and development over the centuries. Scripture in the Acts of the Apostles documents deep and immediate conversions and Baptisms (Acts 2:14–41, 8:26–39). Baptism marked a change of heart and conversion to a way of life that was lived in community. Later the process of initiation took on a more structured approach in the development of the baptismal catechumenate where those who were looking to become Christian were apprenticed, as it were, to the community for what could be a lengthy period of time. They were baptized when they and the community discerned that their lifestyle had changed and they were living for Christ. Inititation into the community took place through the reception of Baptism, Confirmation, and Eucharist, which were celebrated in the same ceremony. The elements of conversion to a way of life and the realization that Baptism forgave all sin often caused people to delay their full initiation until the end of their lives.

Confirmation

Write the word *Confirmation* on the board or on chart paper.

- Explain that this sacrament strengthens baptized persons with the gifts of the Holy Spirit.

- Read the prayers from the text, and ask children which Person of the Trinity we receive in a special way during Confirmation. **the Holy Spirit**

- Have children find the photograph of the Confirmation celebration.

- Explain what is happening in the picture. **The boy is being confirmed.**

Eucharist

Write the word *Eucharist* on the board or on chart paper.

- Read the text aloud. Clarify that *Eucharist* is a name used for the whole action of the Mass and that *Holy Communion* is the receiving of the Body and Blood of Jesus during the Eucharist.

- Point out the photograph of the child receiving Holy Communion.

❷ Discuss the question to review the Sacraments of Initiation. **Possible answers: They make us members of the Church; Baptism and Confirmation mark us as God's children.**

Review

- Baptism, Confirmation, and Eucharist are the Sacraments of Initiation.

- These sacraments make us full members of the Church.

- These sacraments are signs that we belong to God.

Objective

To help children express that they are followers of Christ

Children of Light

Respond

Explain that *Child of the Light* means "a person who follows Jesus." Read the directions to children.

- Help children think of words that describe a follower of Jesus.

- Have children complete the activity.

- If necessary, help children spell the words.

Closing Blessing

- Gather children into a prayer circle with their books.

- Begin with the Sign of the Cross.

- Read aloud the People of Faith story about Blessed Carlos Manuel Rodríguez.

- Pray the prayer.

End by leading children in singing *Songs of Celebration* CD, track 7, "Yes Lord, I Believe!" or one of the optional music suggestions on page 3.

Children of Light

Respond

Describe a disciple In the banner below, color in the words "Child of the Light." Then write words that describe a follower of Jesus.

Child of the Light

_____

_____

_____

10

Closing Blessing

Gather and begin with the Sign of the Cross.

Leader: God, our Father, we thank you for choosing us to be your children.

All: Amen.

Leader: Jesus, the Son of God, we thank you for showing us how to live.

All: Amen.

Leader: Holy Spirit, giver of God's gifts, we praise and thank you for guiding us.

Sing together.

I believe in God the Father
I believe in God the Son
I believe in the Spirit
And the strength that makes us one.

© 2000 John Burland

 People of Faith: A Read Aloud Story

Blessed Carlos Manuel Rodríguez

Blessed Carlos Manuel Rodríguez was born in Puerto Rico on November 22, 1918. His friends called him "Charlie." Charlie wanted to help people do things to make the world more Christian. During his life he spent a lot of time gathering people into study groups. He thought it was important for all baptized people to be involved in spreading the faith. He also spent time translating English liturgy into Spanish so that the members of the Church in Puerto Rico could pray in their own language. Charlie's belief in the Resurrection of Jesus was very important to his life. Because of this, the Easter Vigil was an important celebration for him.

C. 1918–1963

Faith at Home

Faith Focus

- A sacrament is a holy sign that comes from Jesus and gives us grace.

- Baptism, Confirmation, and Eucharist are called Sacraments of Initiation.

- The Sacraments of Initiation make us full members of the Church.

Ritual Focus

Renewal of Baptismal Promises

The celebration focused on the Renewal of Baptismal Promises. The children renewed their baptismal promises. During the week, use the text on pages 2–3, and renew your own baptism promises with your child and the rest of the family.

www.harcourtreligion.com
Visit our Web site for weekly scripture readings and questions, family resources, and more activities.

Act

Share Together Read John 15:1–17. Talk about what actions show we are friends of Jesus. Using a shoe box, create a "Friends of Jesus" box. Invite family members to look for examples of how others are acting as friends of Jesus, write the examples on pieces of paper, and place them in the box. At the end of the week, read the slips of paper and share what you have learned.

Do Together When discussing your child's Baptism, talk about all of the things you did to prepare for his or her birth. Point out that some babies are born into families who do not have the means to prepare for them. Discuss what you and your child could do to help. (Suggestions: Buy baby food or diapers for a homeless shelter, or pray for these children at a specific time every day.)

Family Prayer

God, our Father, thank you for making us your children. We believe in you and we belong to you. We ask you to keep us close to you. Show us how to love each other as you have loved us. Amen.

11

Faith at Home

Review the five parts of the Faith at Home page with children.

Encourage children:

- to ask family members to review the **Faith Focus** statements

- to share the **Ritual Focus: Renewal of Baptismal Promises** with family members

- to do at least one of the **Act** activities with family members

- to pray the **Family Prayer** with their family at times when the family is together

- to encourage their family members to go to **www.harcourtreligion.com** with them and do the activities for this chapter sometime during the week

Looking Ahead

For Chapter 2, you will need:

- a Bible

- a prayer table

- a candle

- a large glass bowl filled with water

- The *Songs of Celebration* CD

- copies of Activity Master 2 on p. CE3 for each child

- copies of Scripture Drama 2 on pp. CE4–5 for participants

General Instruction of the Roman Missal

"Their purpose (the rites preceding the Liturgy of the Word) is to ensure that the faithful who come together as one establish communion and dispose themselves to listen properly to God's word and to celebrate the Eucharist worthily." (no. 46)

Catechism Connection

To deepen your own background and reflection on the Introductory Rites, refer to the *Catechism of the Catholic Church,* 1153, 1156–1158.

Catechist Resources

 The Breaking of the Bread: The Development of the Eucharist According to Acts
Eugene Laverdiere
Liturgical Training Publications
Presents an understanding of the Eucharist by examining the life of the early Church

 Saving Signs, Wondrous Words
David Philippart
Liturgical Training Publications
Explains twenty-five words, actions, gestures, signs, and symbols of the liturgy in short essays

Children's Resources

 Prayer of Praise (10 min)
St. Anthony Messenger Press
Encourages young people to have an attitude of praise as they experience a story, a praise walk, and a guided meditation

 Our Church
Graham English
Liturgical Press
Uses children's stories to show how children connect to the Church through prayer and ritual

 * *Available at* **www.harcourtreligion.com**

Catechist Formation

> "For where two or three are gathered together in my name, there am I in the midst of them."
>
> Matthew 18:20

The Importance of Gathering

The difference between an anonymous crowd on a street and sports fans in a football stadium is that the sports fans are gathered with a common purpose: to cheer on their team. Similarly, when Catholics gather for Mass, they gather as one family who shares a common faith and purpose.

The purpose of the entrance song is twofold "to foster the unity of those who have been gathered" and "to introduce their thoughts to the mystery of the liturgical season or festivity" (*General Instruction of the Roman Missal,* 47). The procession expresses that we are a "pilgrim people."

The opening prayer of the Mass is called the collect. The priest gathers together or collects the petitions of the community and offers them to God. The prayer also prepares people to listen attentively to God's word and to give thanks to God for all that he has accomplished throughout history.

The Presence of Christ

The gathering of the assembly at Mass is one of the signs that Christ is truly present. This presence of Christ is also seen in the priest who presides, the word proclaimed, and, most especially, in the consecrated bread and wine, which is the Body and Blood of Jesus. By gathering as the Body of Christ, the members of the assembly are strengthened to live faithfully following the examples of the Christian communities (*Acts 2:42–47*).

What signs do you see in your parish that the community is truly gathering as one?

What role do you have in helping the community to gather for prayer?

Catechist Prayer

Holy God, lead me to be one with my brothers and sisters in faith. May our gatherings of prayer help me see you in our midst. Amen.

Lesson Planner

		OBJECTIVES	LESSON PROCESS	✹ ACTIVITIES	MATERIALS
CELEBRATE	15 minutes Pages 12–13	Ritual Focus *Procession and Gloria* To experience a celebration of the word, including a procession and the singing of the Gloria	Celebrate the opening prayer.		PROGRAM RESOURCES *Songs of Celebration* CD, track 8 OTHER MATERIALS Bible, prayer table, candle, large glass bowl filled with water
	Pages 14–15	To explore the meaning of the ritual actions To teach about the ways the community comes together and prays during the Mass	Reflect on the celebration. Complete the activity. ✝ Read about and discuss the role of the assembly. ✝ Read about and discuss gathering for worship. Describe how processions are part of our worship.	✹ **Reflect** Children draw pictures of thanks and praise.	
REMEMBER	30 minutes Pages 16–17	Faith Focus *What is a community of faith?* To understand the qualities of a community of faith	Discuss why we are a community of faith. 📖 Proclaim the scripture story. *Acts 2:42–47* Complete the activity.	✹ **Share** Partners write and perform a play. **Faith at Home** Suggested activities for the home	PROGRAM RESOURCES Copies of Activity Master 2, p. CE3 Copies of Scripture Drama 2, pp. CE4–5 OTHER MATERIALS Props for dramatizing the Gospel story
	Pages 18–19	Faith Focus *What happens when we gather as a community of faith?* To describe the Introductory Rites	Discuss the importance of the Introductory Rites. Examine why we worship together. ✝ Read about and discuss the importance of prayer and singing.	**Faith at Home** Suggested activities for the home	
LIVE	15 minutes Page 20	To model ways of praising God	Introduce the activity. Pray the Closing Blessing. Read aloud the People of Faith story about Sister Thea Bowman.	✹ **Respond** Children list reasons to praise and thank God.	PROGRAM RESOURCES *Songs of Celebration* CD, track 8
FAITH AT HOME	Page 21	**Faith at Home** To introduce the different parts of the Faith at Home page	Review the Faith at Home page. Encourage children to share this page at home.	✹ **Act** Suggested activities for the home	PROGRAM RESOURCES Family Guide, pp. 18–19

CELEBRATE

Objective

To experience a celebration of the word, including a procession and the singing of the Gloria

Preparation

Familiarize yourself with the movements of the ritual focus for the Procession and Gloria on pages 12–13.

Prepare the prayer space ahead of time. You will need:

- a Bible
- a table covered with a white cloth
- a candle and a large glass bowl filled with water on the prayer table
- Use the *Songs of Celebration* CD, track 8, to rehearse the suggested song, "Glory to God," or one of the optional music suggestions on page 13.

Select a child to carry the Bible in procession.

We Gather

Invite children to assemble with their books.

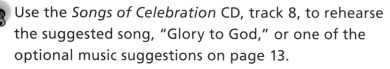

Ritual Focus: Procession and Gloria

Gather children into the prayer space with a procession.

- Direct children to follow you and the child carrying the Bible, as you lead the procession.
- As you process, lead the children in singing using the *Songs of Celebration* CD, track 8.
- When all are assembled, light the prayer candle.
- Begin prayer, and lead the children in the Sign of the Cross.

Follow the order of prayer on pages 12–13.

Chapter **2** **We Gather**

CELEBRATE

We Gather

Ritual Focus: Procession and Gloria

As you sing, walk forward slowly.
Follow the person carrying the Bible.

 Sing together.

Glory to God in the highest,
and peace to his people on earth.
Glory to God in the highest,
and peace to his people on earth.

©1987 GIA Publications, Inc.

Leader: Let us pray.

Make the Sign of the Cross together.

God, our Loving Father, we praise you for your goodness and thank you for the gift of your Son, Jesus. Send us your Holy Spirit to help us live as your children. We ask this through Jesus Christ our Lord.

All: Amen.

Leader: Every Sunday we come together as God's people to praise him and to give him thanks for everything he has done. Today we do the same.

Come forward, and gather around the holy water and candle.

Lord Jesus, you came to gather all people into your Father's kingdom.

All: We give you glory and thanks.

Leader: Lord Jesus, you came to bring us new life.

12

✦ Liturgical Background

The Gloria   The first historical record of the Gloria is found in Greek and Syrian sources. It began as an Easter hymn, which became a regular part of Morning Prayer in the Eastern churches.

The Eastern churches were those that looked to Constantinople rather than Rome as their center. Churches that looked to Rome as their center are called the Western churches.

In the sixth century the Gloria entered the Roman Rite. Only the bishops sang it as they presided on Sundays and at the feasts of martyrs. However, priests sang the Gloria at the Easter Vigil. It was not until the eleventh century that the Gloria became a regular part of the Sunday liturgy for all.

It remains a regular part of the liturgy today. The Gloria, sung only on Sundays, solemnities, and special feasts, except in Advent and Lent, is a beautiful reminder of the glory of Easter and the triumph of the Lamb of God.

All: We give you glory and thanks.

Leader: Lord Jesus, you came to save us.

All: We give you glory and thanks.

Leader: Let us give praise and thanks to God.

We Listen

Leader: God, our Father, you alone are holy. We ask you to help us be grateful children who always remember your glory. We ask this through Jesus Christ our Lord.

All: Amen.

Leader: A reading from the Acts of the Apostles.

Read Acts 2:42–47.

The word of the Lord.

All: Thanks be to God.

Sit silently.

We Go Forth

Leader: God, the Holy Spirit, we praise you and thank you for your gifts. May we act in ways that show your gifts to others. We ask this through Jesus Christ our Lord.

All: Amen.

 Sing the opening song together.

13

We Listen

For the proclamation of the Gospel, you may use a Bible or the adapted reading in the *Child's Book* on pages 16–17.

We Go Forth

• Lead the closing prayer. As children process back to their seats, have them sing *Songs of Celebration* CD, track 8, "Glory to God," or one of the optional music suggestions.

Optional Music Suggestions:

"Gloria," © Bob Hurd. Published by OCP

"Pan de vida," © Jaime Cortez. Published by OCP

Ritual Background

Sung parts of the Mass   Some parts of the liturgy are intended to be sung by the people, if at all possible. The Church does not consider singing at the liturgy to be only for those who have special musical talents, but rather it is a profound way for the entire people to express their prayer.

Singing fosters communal prayer and raises the heart to God. According to Saint Augustine, "Singing is for one who loves." There is a difference between singing songs and hymns at Mass and singing the parts of the Mass.

Although both are important, the Church gives greater priority to singing the parts of the Mass, such as the Gloria; the Gospel Acclamation; the Holy, Holy, Holy; the Memorial Acclamation; the Amen that concludes the Eucharistic Prayer; and the Lamb of God. By singing, we intensify our participation in the Eucharist.

Objective

To explore the meaning of the ritual actions of procession and the singing of the Gloria

To teach about the ways the community comes together and prays during the Mass

Liturgical Catechesis

The purpose of this section is to help children reflect on their experiences of the signs, rituals, prayers, and gestures of the celebration and to lead them to express their own meaning of the experiences. Allow children to share their experiences without commenting on them.

Gathered Together

- On the board or on chart paper, write the following questions: What did you see? What did you hear? What did you do?

- Guide children to reflect on the celebration by reviewing what happened in the prayer.

- Invite children to share their responses.

Reflect

- Invite children to think about something for which they want to give God thanks and praise. Have them draw a picture of this in their books.

- Have volunteers share their responses.

Assembly

- Read aloud the text.
- Talk about the different times people come together.
- Ask children to name what happens when people come together. They are friendly; they do things together.
- Point out that when we come together as people who believe in Jesus, we do many of the same things.

Gathered Together

SIGNS OF FAITH

Assembly
Many different people come together at Mass. Each person comes to praise and give thanks to God and to ask for his blessings. When we gather together to give God thanks and praise, we are an **assembly** of people who believe in Jesus. When the assembly gathers, God is there.

Reflect

Procession and Gloria   Draw a picture of what you want to thank and praise God for.

Additional Activity

Write a cinquain   Explain to children that a cinquain is a poem made up of five lines. Together with children, write a cinquain about one of the following: the Gloria, the procession, or the gathering.

- Prepare a large sheet of paper or a space on the board ahead of time.

- Mark off five lines.

- On the first line, write a one-word title for the subject of your cinquain.

- Ask children for two descriptive words about the title, and place them on the second line.

- Repeat the process for three action words about the title. Place them on the third line.

- Repeat the process for a four-word phrase about the subject. Place it on the fourth line.

- Repeat the process for one or two words that describe the title. Place them on the fifth line.

Have children recite the cinquain together.

We Come Together

Every time we gather as a group, we come together to pray. When we begin to form the **procession** for our celebration, we are gathering for prayer. **Prayer** is talking and listening to God. The procession gathers us as a community ready for prayer.

During the Mass, we pray in many different ways. When we stand, we pray a prayer of reverence. Prayers can be said. We can say the Lord Have Mercy. We can ask for God's help. Prayers can be sung. We can sing the Glory to God in Mass. We pray in silence during the Mass, too. One time we pray in silence is after the Gospel reading.

SIGNS OF FAITH

Procession

A procession is a group of people moving forward as part of a celebration. Processions at Mass remind us that we are walking with God and that God is walking with us. At Mass the priest and other ministers come into the church in a procession. People bring the gifts to the altar in a procession. We walk in a procession to receive Jesus in Holy Communion.

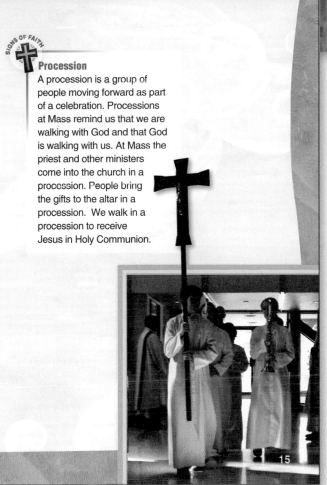

We Come Together

- Ask children to read the first paragraph silently. Tell them to find the sentence that tells what prayer is. talking and listening to God

- Summarize the second paragraph. Explain how we pray in different ways with words (the Sign of the Cross), in silence, by singing, and with gesture (the procession).

Procession

- Invite several children to read the text aloud.

- Remind children that they were in a procession at the beginning of the celebration in this session and the previous one. Explain that all these celebrations have a procession.

- Invite children to pay attention to the processions during Sunday Mass.

Teaching Tip

Greeting in the classroom   Use the Introductory Rites as a model for greeting children as they arrive. Arrive early and stand by the door. As children enter the classroom, try to engage them by:

- greeting them as individuals

- giving them time to greet one another

- asking them to assist you with preparing the room for class

- having a gathering activity prepared

- clearly showing when class is beginning with a special gesture or phrase

Objective

To understand the qualities of a community of faith

Faith Focus

What is a community of faith?

List children's responses on the board or on chart paper.

We Gather as God's People

Write the word *community* on the board or on chart paper. Elicit from children the different communities to which they belong.

- Call attention to the illustration of an early Christian community. Have children point out the similarities to a Church gathering today.

- As you summarize the text, emphasize that early Christians were drawn together because of their love of Jesus.

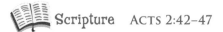

Scripture ACTS 2:42–47

The Early Christians

- Gather children into a story circle or in the prayer space. Remind them that they will be hearing the story from the Acts of the Apostles again.

- Ask what they remember from hearing the story during the celebration.

- Reread the story aloud.

- Or, select some children to dramatize the story. Use the text on pages CE4–5 of this edition.

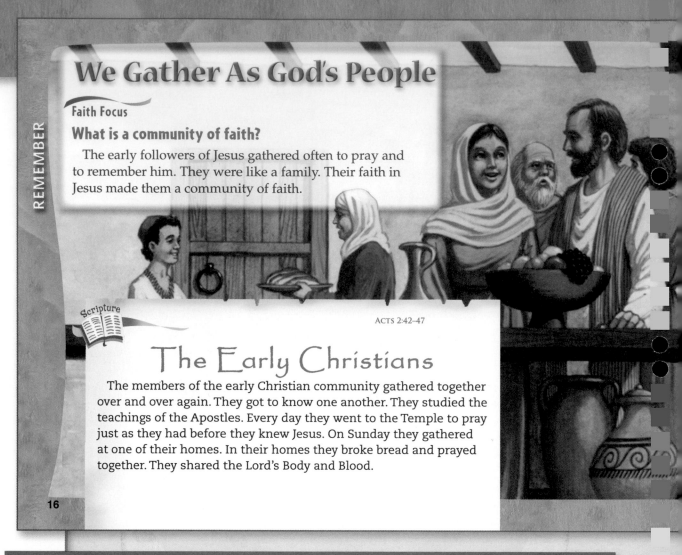

REMEMBER

We Gather As God's People

Faith Focus

What is a community of faith?

The early followers of Jesus gathered often to pray and to remember him. They were like a family. Their faith in Jesus made them a community of faith.

Scripture ACTS 2:42–47

The Early Christians

The members of the early Christian community gathered together over and over again. They got to know one another. They studied the teachings of the Apostles. Every day they went to the Temple to pray just as they had before they knew Jesus. On Sunday they gathered at one of their homes. In their homes they broke bread and prayed together. They shared the Lord's Body and Blood.

16

Scripture Background

Breaking of the Bread The reading in Acts describes the relationships and life of the early Christian community. The description of the early Christians gathering together in their homes for the "breaking of the bread" shows that they wanted to remain faithful to Jesus' command "Do this in memory of me" and the importance of Sunday as "the first day of the week."

According to Luke *(Luke 24:35; Acts 2:42; 20:11)*, the Christians called this meal the "breaking of the bread." Paul refers to this celebration as the "Lord's supper" *(1 Cor. 11:20)* and warns the Christians in Corinth not to let their household

gatherings for food and drink do "more harm than good." He reminds them that the reason for their gathering was primarily to observe the Lord's Supper in memory of what Jesus did the night before he died. From then until now we continue to celebrate the Sacrament of the Eucharist throughout the whole Church with the same fundamental structure.

The early followers of Jesus shared their belongings with one another. They sold their property and possessions and made sure everyone had what they needed. Every time they ate together, they gave praise and thanks to God. They were very joyful. When other people saw how happy the followers of Jesus were, they wanted to join their community. They wanted to believe in Jesus and follow him.

BASED ON ACTS 2:42–47

 How were the early Christians a community of faith?

 How is your Church a community of faith?

Faith at Home

Read the scripture story with your child. Explain that many early Christians were Jewish and went to the Temple. Point out that the early Christians did not have church buildings. Talk about the ways your family and parish take care of the needs of other Christians.

Share

Write a play With a partner, prepare a play showing one thing you do because you belong to a community of faith. Act out the play for the class.

17

- Discuss how others felt when they saw how happy the Christians were. They wanted to become part of the Church community.

 Discuss the question. They believed in Jesus; they knew each other; they broke bread and prayed together.

 Discuss the question. Possible responses: they help the poor; they gather for Mass; they have coffee and donuts after Mass.

Share

- Organize children into pairs for the activity.
- Explain the activity to children, and tell them how much time they have to work.
- Begin the activity, and circulate through the group to assist where you are needed.
- Have children share their plays with the class.

Activity Master

You may wish to use Activity Master 2 on page CE3 to further integrate the meaning of the Gospel story.

▲ Activity Master 2

Review

- Early Christians met in communities of faith.
- We belong to a community of faith.

✴ Cultural Background

Separation In the society of Jesus' day, only people of the same social status shared meals with one another. Men ate separately from women, freedmen separated from slaves, Jews from Gentiles, rich from poor. Even the food that they ate distinguished social classes.

Paul emphasizes that there ought not to exist among Christians the divisions that ordinary society tolerated and sometimes even encouraged *(1 Corinthians 11:17–34).*

- Christians represented a whole new society, different from anything previously known.

- In the "new creation" called the Church, all are one "in Christ." There is neither "Jew nor Greek, there is neither slave nor free person, there is not male and female" *(Galatians 3:28).*

- Such distinctions were not to characterize Christians or Christian assemblies.

Objective

To describe the Introductory Rites

Faith Focus

What happens when we gather as a community of faith?

List children's responses on the board or on chart paper.

The People Gather

Recall the procession that started the celebration at the beginning of the session. Point out that our Saturday night or Sunday Masses begin with a procession, too.

- Have children read aloud the reasons for worshiping together each weekend.

- Have children recall what happens when we gather for Mass. We greet one another, sing, and pray.

Prayer and Singing

- Read aloud the text.

- Discuss the meaning of singing at celebrations.

- Invite children to share times when they sing with family members or friends.

- If possible, bring hymnals to class and familiarize children with them.

- You may also want to invite your music minister to talk about how music is selected for Mass or, if there is a children's choir, to invite children to participate.

The People Gather

SIGNS OF FAITH

Prayer and Singing

Singing is a way to pray. When we sing during Mass, we lift our minds, hearts, and voices to praise God in a special way. The whole assembly sings songs and hymns. Sometimes the choir sings and the assembly listens. The priest sometimes sings parts of the Mass.

Faith Focus

What happens when we gather as a community of faith?

Like the first Christians, we celebrate the Eucharist with a community, too. Our faith community is our Church family. During Mass we come together as the Body of Christ. Every Saturday evening or Sunday, we gather with our parish community for the celebration of Mass.

Sunday is an important day for Christians. Jesus rose from the dead on Easter Sunday. It is so important that the Church requires us to participate in Sunday Mass every week. We come together as an assembly on Sunday to give God thanks and praise, to listen to God's word, and to ask for his blessing. We also remember Jesus' death, Resurrection, and Ascension and share the Lord's Body and Blood. Then we are sent forth to live as Jesus' followers.

When we gather for Mass, we greet one another. We share our joy as we sing and pray.

18

✦ Catechist Background

Sunday In ancient pagan times, the first day of the week was called Sunday because it honored the sun. Christians began to call Sunday the Lord's Day, primarily to remember that Jesus rose from the dead on Easter Sunday.

From the beginning, Sunday replaced the Jewish Sabbath as the Christian day of worship. Since the Jewish calendar marked days from sundown to sundown, the Jewish Sabbath began on Friday evening at sundown and continued until sundown on Saturday. The recent Catholic practice of celebrating the Sunday Eucharist on Saturday afternoon and evening has some precedent in the Jewish Sabbath.

Besides participating in the celebration of the Eucharist on Sundays, Catholics are also called to keep the Lord's Day holy by prayer, works of charity, and relaxation from work.

Introductory Rites

The prayers and actions that begin the Mass are called the Introductory Rites. The Introductory Rites help us turn our hearts and minds to the great celebration of the Eucharist. The priest leads the assembly in the celebration of the Mass. Mass begins when he walks in procession to the altar. All of us in the assembly stand and sing.

The priest greets us. He often says "The Lord be with you," or similar words. We answer "And also with you." We know that God the Father, his Son, Jesus, and the Holy Spirit are with us. We believe Jesus is present in every part of the Mass. Together we thank God for his goodness.

❓ How do we show we are united as we gather for the Mass?

Faith at Home

Discuss responses to the question. Talk about which songs sung during Mass are your favorites. If you have the *Songs of Celebration* CD for this program, spend some time listening to the songs. Use this page to go over the Introductory Rites. Review the responses with your child.

19

⁕ Sacrament Background

Structure of the Mass Roman Catholic worship has its roots in Judaism and the New Testament. From earliest times the focus of liturgy was the assembly gathering to remember the celebration of Jesus' Last Supper. These gatherings always had some structure but not as formal a structure as we experience today.

Over the centuries the Mass developed different forms and was affected by the architecture of churches and the influx of different cultures.

In the sixteenth century the Council of Trent revised the Roman liturgy and made it uniform for the whole Western Church. The structure of the Mass, which developed from this reform, was maintained until the Second Vatican Council (1962), which called for a renewal of all the rites of the Church. Some of the changes in the Mass included the priest facing the people, more participation of the people, the use of vernacular language, and a renewed emphasis on Scripture.

Introductory Rites

Write the word *Introductory Rites* on the board or on chart paper.

- Summarize the first paragraph. Point out that during the Introductory Rites, we greet one another and begin our worship by praising God with songs, prayers, and actions.

- Invite children to look at the photographs on pages 20 and 21 and tell what they see.

- Read aloud the second paragraph, and practice the response with children. Point out that the priest and people speak to one another during the Introductory Rites.

- ❓ Discuss the question. Show how the people become one during worship. We greet one another, stand together, and pray and sing together.

Review

- The Introductory Rites begin the Mass.
- We pray and sing together as Mass begins.

Objective

To model ways of praising God

Give Praise and Thanks

Respond

Explain the activity to children. Suggest that they include the following in their list:

- people
- places
- things
- feelings

Closing Blessing

- Gather children in a prayer circle with their books.
- Begin with the Sign of the Cross.
- Read aloud the People of Faith story about Sister Thea Bowman.
- Pray the prayer.
- End by leading children in singing *Songs of Celebration* CD, track 8, "Glory to God," or one of the optional music suggestions on page 13.

LIVE

Give Praise and Thanks

Respond

Make a list In the space below, make a list of reasons you want to give God praise and thanks.

1. _____

2. _____

3. _____

Closing Blessing

Gather and begin with the Sign of the Cross.

Leader: God, our Father, we praise and thank you for gathering us as your children. Send us your Holy Spirit to increase our faith and make our community strong.

We ask this in the name of Jesus Christ our Lord.

All: Amen.

Leader: Go in peace to love and serve the Lord.

All: Thanks be to God.

Sing together.

Glory to God in the highest,
and peace to his people on earth.
Glory to God in the highest,
and peace to his people on earth.

©1987 GIA Publications, Inc.

20

✸ People of Faith: A Read Aloud Story

Sister Thea Bowman   Thea was born in Canton, Mississippi. Her grandfather was a slave, and her father was a doctor. She was the first African American woman to receive her doctorate in theology from Boston College. Using song, dance, poetry, and stories, Sister Thea helped African American Catholics, both children and adults, put together celebrations of the Mass that expressed the life, joy, and story of their culture.

C. 1937–1990

Faith at Home

Faith Focus
- The Church is the People of God and the Body of Christ.
- The Eucharist, or Mass, is the Church's most important action of praise and thanks.
- The Introductory Rites gather us as a community of faith.

Ritual Focus
Procession and Gloria

The celebration focused on the Procession and Gloria. The children sang the Gloria and prayed a litany of glory and praise to God. During the week, pray and talk about the meaning of the verses of the Gloria found on page 12.

Act

Share Together Read Acts 2:42–47. Talk about what it must have been like for the early Christians to live as a community of faith. Emphasize the sharing of their possessions and their prayer life. Decide one way your family can continue to live as a community of faith, such as going to Mass or sharing your time and talents with others.

Pray Together Together, make a list of all the things you want to thank God for. Read the list as a litany. One person prays, "For sun and rain," and everyone responds, "We thank you, God." During the weeks ahead, select appropriate times to pray a thanksgiving prayer with your child or family.

Litany

Family Prayer
Loving God, we are your people. Thank you for the gift of faith. Help us grow closer as a family. Strengthen our faith in you. Amen.

www.harcourtreligion.com
Visit our Web site for weekly scripture readings and questions, family resources, and more activities.

21

Faith at Home

Review the five parts of the Faith at Home page with children.

Encourage children:

- to ask family members to review the **Faith Focus** statements

- to share the **Ritual Focus: Procession and Gloria** with family members

- to do at least one of the **Act** activities with family members

- to pray the **Family Prayer** with their family at times when the family is together

- to encourage their family members to go to **www.harcourtreligion.com** with them and do the activities for this chapter sometime during the week

Looking Ahead

For Chapter 3, you will need:

- a Bible

- a prayer table

- a candle

- a large glass bowl filled with water

- The *Songs of Celebration* CD

- copies of Activity Master 3 on p. CE6 for each child

- copies of Scripture Drama 3 on pp. CE7–8 for participants

General Instruction of the Roman Missal

"Then the priest invites those present to take part in the Act of Penitence, which, after a brief pause for silence, the entire community carries out through a formula of general confession. The rite concludes with the priest's absolution, which, however, lacks the efficacy of the Sacrament of Penance...." (no. 51)

Catechism Connection

To deepen your own background and reflection on the Eucharist as a Sacrament of Forgiveness, refer to the *Catechism of the Catholic Church, 1393–1395.*

Catechist Resources

 Eucharist Sourcebook*
J. Robert Baker and Barbara Budde
Liturgical Training Publications
Gathers poetry and prose, hymns, and prayers for a reflection on the Eucharist

 We Shall Go Up with Joy: The Entrance Rite *(30 min)*
Liturgical Training Publications
Shows how the Entrance Rite unifies a community as the liturgy begins

Children's Resources

 Bless This House: A Bedtime Prayer for the World*
Leslie Staub
Harcourt
Weaves forgiveness and other comforting themes throughout a bedtime prayer

 The Story of Ruby Bridges
Robert Coles
Scholastic, Inc.
The true story of how one six-year-old girl forgave those who showed her hatred and prejudice

 * *Available at* **www.harcourtreligion.com**

Catechist Formation

> "'... I desire mercy, not sacrifice.'
> I did not come to call the righteous
> but sinners."
>
> Matthew 9:13

Penitential Rite: Ritual of Unity

Most people have had experiences when things are just not right between them and another person. It may be something as trivial as the way the other person uses a tube of toothpaste, or as serious as a betrayal of trust. Whatever the cause, the relationship is disrupted. But then something happens—an unexpected kind word, or a tragedy and a sense of shared humanity, and unity is recovered.

Whenever a community gathers for the Eucharist, the members share the need for God's mercy and love. We are a Church of sinners, and we know it. We come to the Eucharist with a sense of our imperfection. We know that in our human condition, we are in need of God's grace and help—in need of having things right again with God and one another.

God's Mercy

The Introductory Rites of the Mass include the Penitential Rite, during which the assembly joins in a general confession and to ask for God's mercy. The whole assembly recalls that God is a loving God who constantly extends to us his mercy and salvation and who unites us. The primary focus of the Penitential Rite is upon God's gift of mercy, not upon human sinfulness. We confess our sinfulness knowing that the Lord is merciful. This belief and realization unites us as an assembly.

What comes to mind when you realize you are not alone as a sinner?

How does the assurance of God's forgiveness help you?

Catechist Prayer

Merciful Lord, look kindly upon me, especially when I fail. Unite me with all my brothers and sisters. May your compassion strengthen me to follow the path of Jesus Christ with devotion and hope. Amen.

Lesson Planner

	OBJECTIVES	LESSON PROCESS	ACTIVITIES	MATERIALS
CELEBRATE — 15 minutes — Pages 22–23	Ritual Focus *Penitential Rite* To experience a celebration of the word, including praying the Confiteor and extending the Sign of Peace	Celebrate the opening prayer.		PROGRAM RESOURCES *Songs of Celebration* CD, track 9 OTHER MATERIALS Bible, prayer table, candle, large glass bowl filled with water
CELEBRATE — Pages 24–25	To explore the meaning of the ritual action To teach the relationship between forgiveness and unity	Reflect on the celebration. Complete the activity. ✝ Read about and discuss the Penitential Rite, including the Lord Have Mercy. Describe the word united. ✝ Read about and discuss silence.	☀ **Reflect** Children reflect on the experience of the celebration and the meaning of the Confiteor.	
REMEMBER — 30 minutes — Pages 26–27	Faith Focus *Why did Jesus eat with sinners?* To explain that Jesus was a friend of sinners	Discuss Jesus' attitude toward sinners. 📖 Proclaim the Gospel story. *Matthew 9:9–13* Complete the activity.	☀ **Share** Children complete a rhyme about Jesus' friendship. 🏠 **Faith at Home** Suggested activities for the home	PROGRAM RESOURCES Copies of Activity Master 3, p. CE6 Copies of Scripture Drama 3, pp. CE7–8 OTHER MATERIALS Props for dramatizing the Gospel story
REMEMBER — Pages 28–29	Faith Focus *What happens during the Penitential Rite?* To explain why we pray for forgiveness at Mass	Identify reasons for asking forgiveness. ✝ Read about and discuss sprinkling with holy water. Examine the Penitential Rite and Confiteor.	🏠 **Faith at Home** Suggested activities for the home	
LIVE — 15 minutes — Page 30	To integrate and review signs and prayers of forgiveness	Introduce the activity. Pray the Closing Blessing. Read aloud the People of Faith story about Pope John Paul II.	☀ **Respond** Children make a bulletin board about forgiveness at home, school, or church.	PROGRAM RESOURCES *Songs of Celebration* CD, track 9
FAITH AT HOME — Page 31	🏠 **Faith at Home** To introduce the different parts of the Faith at Home page	Review the Faith at Home page. Encourage children to share this page at home.	☀ **Act** Suggested activities for the home	PROGRAM RESOURCES Family Guide, pp. 20–21

CELEBRATE

Objective

To experience a celebration of the word, including the Penitential Rite

Preparation

Familiarize yourself with the movements of the ritual focus for the Confiteor and extending the Sign of Peace on pages 22–23. You will need:

- a table covered with a white cloth
- a Bible
- a candle and a large glass bowl filled with water on the prayer table

 Use the *Songs of Celebration* CD, track 9, to rehearse the suggested song, "Psalm 51: Create in Me," or one of the optional music suggestions on page 23.

We Gather

- Gather children into a prayer circle.
- When all are assembled, light the prayer candle.
- Lead children in singing using the *Songs of Celebration* CD, track 9.
- Begin prayer, and lead the children in the Sign of the Cross.

Follow the order of prayer on pages 22–23.

Ritual Focus: Penitential Rite

- Invite children to sit as they reflect.
- Ask children to stand for the Confiteor.

We Are Forgiven

CELEBRATE

We Gather

Ritual Focus: Penitential Rite

🎵 Sing together.

Create in me a clean heart, O God.

A clean heart, O God, create in me.

©Tom Kendzia

Leader: Let us pray.

Make the Sign of the Cross together.

Confiteor

Leader: God wants us to be united with him. Let us think about the times we have not been united to God or others.

Sit silently.

Leader: Let us pray for God's forgiveness and mercy.

Come forward, and gather around the holy water and candle.

All: I confess to almighty God, and to you, my brothers and sisters, that I have sinned through my own fault in my thoughts and in my words, in what I have done, and in what I have failed to do; and I ask blessed Mary, ever virgin, all the angels and saints, and you, my brothers and sisters, to pray for me to the Lord our God.

Leader: May God forgive us our sins and make us united with him and one another.

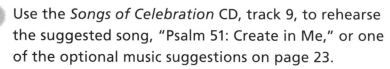

22

✴ Liturgical Background

The Penitential Rite In the opening rites of Mass there are three options for The Penitential Rite. One of these includes the prayer called the Confiteor, which is the Latin word for "I confess."

To understand the Confiteor, it is important to see how this prayer fits into the whole action of the Penitential Rite. First, the priest invites the people into a spirit of recollection. Next, there is a moment of silence. Only after the moment of silence is the Confiteor prayed by all. The people must be given time to reflect before they can pray this prayer of confession. Finally, the priest says the absolution. (*Sacramentary*, p. 360) It is not a sacramental absolution, as we find in the Sacrament of Penance, but a simple invocation of God's mercy.

The Penitential Rite assures that whenever we gather for Mass we are called to enter into a spirit of recollection. Remembering we are sinners and asking forgiveness, we realize our needs for God, who is generous ad merciful.

We Listen

Leader: God, our loving Father, you call us to forgiveness and peace. You want us to be united in you. Help us forgive others as you forgive us. We ask this through Jesus Christ our Lord.

All: Amen.

Leader: A reading from the holy Gospel according to Matthew.

All: Glory to you, Lord.

Leader: Read Matthew 9:9–13.

The Gospel of the Lord.

All: Praise to you, Lord Jesus Christ.

Sit silently.

We Go Forth

Leader: Let us offer each other the Sign of Peace.

Give the Sign of Peace to one another.
Say: "The Peace of the Lord be with you."
Answer: "And also with you."

Go forth united in God's love.

All: Amen.

 Sing the opening song together.

23

We Listen

For the proclamation of the Gospel, you may use a Bible or the adapted reading in the *Child's Book* on pages 26–27.

We Go Forth

Lead the closing prayer. As children process back to their seats, have them sing *Songs of Celebration* CD, track 9, "Psalm 51: Create in Me" or one of the optional music suggestions.

 Optional Music Suggestions:

Salmo 50: "Oh Dios, crea en mí," © Eleazar Cortés. Published by OCP

"Loving and Forgiving," © Scott Soper. Published by OCP

✦ Ritual Background

General Confession   The Confiteor is not addressed to God alone, but also "to you, my brothers and sisters." It is a general prayer of confession for each person to acknowledge publicly, before God and the community, that he or she is a person who needs forgiveness. This act of humility creates a bond among those who join together in worship. We admit, as Saint Paul did, that "all have sinned, and are deprived of the glory of God" *(Romans 3:23)*.

At the conclusion of the Confiteor, in another gesture of solidarity, we ask our brothers and sisters to pray for us. The prayers of Mary, the saints in heaven, and our Church family help us to approach God with confidence in his mercy.

CELEBRATE

Objective

To explore the meaning of the ritual action of praying the Confiteor

To teach the relationship between forgiveness and unity

Liturgical Catechesis

The purpose of this section is to help children reflect on their experiences of the signs, rituals, prayers, and gestures of the celebration and to lead them to express their own meaning of the experiences. Allow children to share their experiences without commenting on them.

God's Forgiveness

- On the board or on chart paper, write the following questions: What did you see? What did you hear? What did you do?

- Guide children to reflect on the celebration by reviewing what happened in the prayer.

Reflect

- Ask children to think about a time when they told a family member or friend that they were sorry and the other person forgave them.

- Make sure children understand the directions.

- Distribute markers and have children draw their pictures.

- Invite volunteers to share their story.

Lord Have Mercy

- Have several volunteers take turns reading aloud the text.

- Tell children that God is always ready to show us his mercy.

God's Forgiveness

CELEBRATE

SIGNS OF FAITH

Lord Have Mercy
Sometimes in the Mass, during the Penitential Rite, we say the prayer Lord Have Mercy. These are the words that people say to Jesus when they ask him to heal them. When we pray these words at Mass, we ask Jesus to heal and forgive our sins and the sins of the world. We want everyone to be forgiven and united to God and one another forever.

Reflect

Confiteor Draw the story of a time when you said, "I am sorry," and the other person said, "I forgive you."

"I am sorry."

"I forgive you."

24

Additional Activity

Read a story Read aloud *The Story of Ruby Bridges* by Robert Coles (Scholastic, Inc., 1995). It is a true and fascinating story about the journey of six-year-old Ruby Bridges, one of three African American children who integrated the New Orleans public school system in 1961. It is a story of faith and forgiveness in the face of hatred and prejudice. The psychologist who accompanied Ruby on the journey authored the book.

We Are One

Just as our parents want our family to be united, or joined together, God wants us to be united to him. When we gather for Mass, we remember that God wants us to love and care for each other.

But sometimes we do not show love to others. In the beginning of the Mass, we say a prayer to show we are sorry. We tell God and the Church family, "I am sorry." We ask forgiveness. We are united with God and our church family.

 SIGNS OF FAITH

Silence

There are special times of quiet at Mass. These times of silence unite us to God. During the silent times, we talk to God in our hearts. We keep our minds and hearts open to what God may be sharing with us.

25

We Are One

- Ask children to share what "being united" or "being together" means to them.

- Have volunteers read aloud the first paragraph.

- Summarize the second paragraph.

- Review the Confiteor on page 22 with children.

- Explain that confessing our sins to God and one another is a sign that we want to be united at the Eucharist.

 Silence

- Ask children how it felt to be silent during the celebration.

- Read aloud the text and talk about the different times that children can be silent and talk to God in their hearts.

 Teaching Tip

Keep it hypothetical Whenever you discuss with children various experiences of sin, be sure to distance the examples from individuals. Do not mention specific children's names or use situations that actually occurred within the group.

If children try to bring up actions of a classmate or a family member, remind them that this is a private issue between the person and God. Emphasize that we should not judge other people's actions as sins.

Objective

To explain that Jesus is a friend to sinners

Faith Focus

Why did Jesus eat with sinners?

List children's responses on the board or on chart paper.

Jesus Calls Sinners

Call attention to the illustration. Have children tell what is happening in it. Jesus is eating with some people.

- Point out that sometimes Jesus ate with people who had turned away from God, or were sinners.

- Summarize the paragraph to show Jesus' attitude toward sinners: He wanted to be friends with them so that they would come to know God and return back to his friendship.

 Scripture   MATTHEW 9:9–13

The Call of Matthew

- Gather children into a story circle or in the prayer space. Remind them that they will be hearing the story from the Gospel of Matthew again.

- Ask what they remember from hearing the Gospel during the celebration.

- Reread the story aloud.

- Or, select some children to dramatize the story. Use the text on pages CE7–8 of this edition.

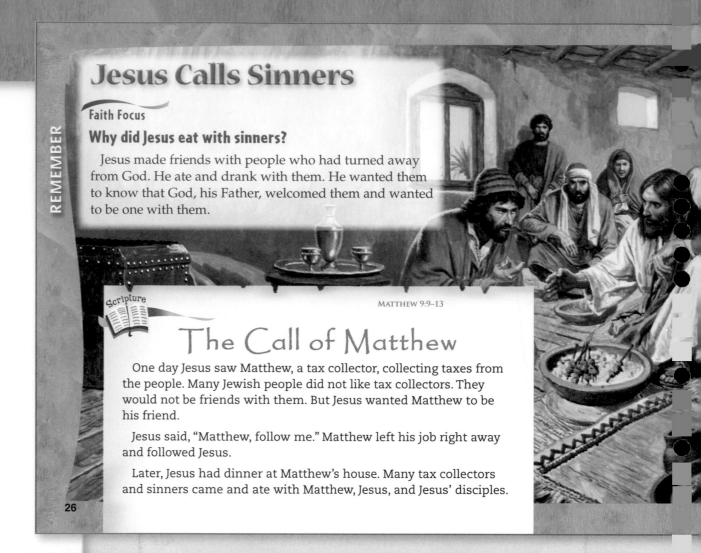

REMEMBER

Jesus Calls Sinners

Faith Focus

Why did Jesus eat with sinners?

Jesus made friends with people who had turned away from God. He ate and drank with them. He wanted them to know that God, his Father, welcomed them and wanted to be one with them.

Scripture   MATTHEW 9:9–13

The Call of Matthew

One day Jesus saw Matthew, a tax collector, collecting taxes from the people. Many Jewish people did not like tax collectors. They would not be friends with them. But Jesus wanted Matthew to be his friend.

Jesus said, "Matthew, follow me." Matthew left his job right away and followed Jesus.

Later, Jesus had dinner at Matthew's house. Many tax collectors and sinners came and ate with Matthew, Jesus, and Jesus' disciples.

26

Scripture Background

Matthew, or Levi   All three synoptic Gospels include the story of the tax collector who was called to follow Jesus and left everything to do so. Only in the Gospel of Matthew is the tax collector named Matthew. In the Gospels of Mark and Luke, he is named Levi *(Mark 2:14–17; Luke 5:27–32)*. This observation illustrates that the very early Christians identified with certain stories that started off as historical events in the life of Jesus and became exemplary stories of faith, even though the names or other details of the story may have changed as the story was passed on.

In the Gospel according to Matthew, the author inserts this event into a series of miracle stories, implying that people are healed by Jesus, not only from physical ailments and diseases, but also from sin.

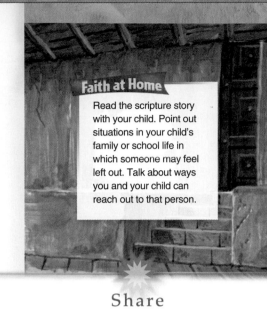

The Pharisees were Jewish leaders and teachers. They saw Jesus eating with sinners and tax collectors. They asked Jesus' disciples, "Why does your teacher eat with these people?"

When Jesus heard their question, he said, "I eat with them because I came to call sinners to be one with my Father."

BASED ON MATHEW 9:9–13

❓ How do you think Matthew felt when Jesus asked him to become a follower?

❓ What do Jesus' words tell you?

Faith at Home

Read the scripture story with your child. Point out situations in your child's family or school life in which someone may feel left out. Talk about ways you and your child can reach out to that person.

Share

Write a rhyme Write a sentence that rhymes with this:

Jesus always welcomes me.

_____

_____

27

- Have children summarize how Jesus felt about Matthew and the people Jesus was eating with.

❓ Invite children to share their responses to the first question. Possible responses: happy, curious, special

❓ Ask the second question, and list children's responses on the board or on chart paper. Possible responses: Jesus welcomes me even when I sin; be kind to those who are different from us; be like Jesus.

- Invite children to be quiet for one to two minutes to think about one way they can follow Jesus' words this week.

Share

- Write the phrase from the text on the board or on chart paper. Explain that children are to write a sentence that rhymes with the sentence in the book.

- You may wish to generate a list of rhyming words for *me.*

- After children have worked individually, have them share their work with the group.

Activity Master

You may wish to use Activity Master 3 on page CE6 to further integrate the meaning of the Gospel story.

▲ Activity Master 3

Review

- Jesus made friends with many people.

- Jesus wanted sinners to know that God welcomed them.

✸ Cultural Background

The Pharisees   The Pharisees were strict observers of Jewish Law and custom. They were students and teachers of the Law, and their role was to help the Jewish people interpret the Law in a way that would preserve their Jewish identity in the midst of a non-Jewish government and economic system.

The Pharisees considered it an abomination to eat or socialize with non-Jews or sinners. They considered tax collectors to be sinners because some of them were dishonest and inflated the amount of the tax in order to

pocket the difference. Whether they were honest or not, tax collectors collaborated with the pagan Roman government and supported it by collecting taxes. Pharisees viewed support of the Romans as an obstacle to having their own nation and religious identity.

Objective

To explain why we pray for forgiveness at Mass

Faith Focus

What happens during the Penitential Rite?

List children's responses on the board or on chart paper.

Penitential Rite

- Point out that everyone sins, or turns away from God. Only Jesus and his mother Mary lived sinless lives.

- Read the bulleted items, and give hypothetical examples of children's actions that might fall into each category.

- Ask children why they think we would want to be closer to God again. Possible responses: because we love God; because God loves us; because we want to be with God.

Sprinkling with Holy Water

- Read aloud the text.

- Use the water from the celebration and, with a small branch or your hands, model a sprinkling rite. Direct children to bless themselves as they are sprinkled.

- Remind children that holy water is available for them to use at the entrance to the parish church.

Penitential Rite

REMEMBER

SIGNS OF FAITH

Sprinkling with Holy Water

During some Sunday Masses, the priest walks through the church and sprinkles the assembly with holy water. The sprinkling reminds us of our Baptism. When the priest does the sprinkling with water, it takes the place of the Penitential Rite.

Faith Focus

What happens during the Penitential Rite?

Like the sinners in Jesus' time, sometimes we need Jesus to call us back to loving his Father.

- We may do things that hurt others.
- We may not do things that help people.
- We may not follow God's law by doing what we know is wrong.

When we do these things, we are not at one with God or others. But when we come to Mass to share a meal with Jesus, Jesus welcomes us. It is a time to become one again with God and others. The Eucharist is a sacrament of forgiveness and unity. However, anyone who has not confessed mortal sins must receive the Sacrament of Penance.

28

✦ Catechist Background

Unity   Unity is an essential element of the Church. We are one because:

- we are children of the same Father

- our founder, Jesus, reconciled all of us through his death on the cross

- the same Holy Spirit dwells in the hearts of all the faithful and guides us to unity

- we have the same pope

- we celebrate the same sacraments

- we have the same Scripture and Church Tradition

Sin and its consequences disrupt the unity in the Church. We are reminded of this at the beginning of every Eucharist as we reflect on sin and its consequences, and we pray for God's mercy. The Penitential Rite is not intended to replace the Sacrament of Reconciliation. Rather, it reminds us of who we are before God and what God is calling us to become through this celebration.

We Are Sorry

After the opening song and greeting, we pray together for God's forgiveness during the Penitential Rite. We ask God to make us one again. The priest invites us to remember our sins and be sorry for them.

We pray the Confiteor, a prayer of sorrow that begins with the words, "I confess." Sometimes we also pray the Lord Have Mercy. When we do this, the priest prays three prayers to Jesus, and we answer him. We pray, "Lord, have mercy, Christ, have mercy, Lord, have mercy." At the end of the Penitential Rite, the priest says this prayer:

"May almighty God have mercy on us, forgive us our sins, and bring us to everlasting life."

After the Penitential Rite, the Holy Spirit continues to unite us as an assembly. The Introductory Rites end. We are now ready to listen to God's word.

? Why do you think the Penitential Rite is important?

Faith at Home

Reinforce with your child the meaning of the Penitential Rite. Use examples from your family of times when someone asked forgiveness of others. Point out that relationships grow and are strengthened when people ask for and receive forgiveness. Use pages 22–23 to help your child learn the responses and prayers for the Penitential Rite.

29

Sacrament Background

The Confiteor   The prayer we say today is one of the oldest elements in the Introductory Rites. Although its form has changed over the centuries, its essential parts have remained until today.

- It began in Rome during the seventh and eighth centuries as a moment of quiet prayer by the pope as he prostrated himself on the floor before coming to the altar in papal liturgies.

- Gradually, the period of silence developed into a prayer and confession spoken in a dialogue by or between the priests and deacons and the people. As the practice of confessing one's sins developed, so did the prayers for God's mercy and absolution.

- Until recently, the Confiteor was accompanied by bodily gestures: from the papal prostration, to bowing, to kneeling, and striking the breast.

We Are Sorry

Read the first few lines of the Confiteor to children.

Recall with them that this prayer was part of the opening celebration and that they often hear it at Mass.

Explain that we begin our time as an assembly by leaving behind our sins.

- We pray the Confiteor to show that we are sinners and we need God's mercy.

- Sometimes we will pray the Lord Have Mercy instead of, or along with, the Confiteor.

- From our prayers God will know that we want his mercy and forgiveness.

? Discuss the question and responses to help children recognize the importance of the Penitential Rite. Possible responses: We admit we are sinners; it unites us to God and one another.

Review

- During the Penitential Rite, we recall our sins.

- During the Penitential Rite, God unites us with himself and others.

Objective

To integrate and review signs and prayers of forgiveness

We Forgive

Respond

Explain the activity to children. Have them think about ways they show forgiveness at home, school, or church.

- Ask children to create their own drawings in their books.

- You may want children to create one bulletin board together.

- Ask children to help you plan how to display their work.

Closing Blessing

- Gather children into a prayer circle with their books.

- Begin with the Sign of the Cross.

- Read aloud the People of Faith story about Pope John Paul II.

- Pray the prayer.

- End with the *Songs of Celebration* CD, track 9, "Psalm 51: Create in Me," or one of the optional music suggestions on page 23.

We Forgive

Respond

Make a bulletin board about ways we forgive at home, school, and at church.

30

Closing Blessing

Gather and begin with the Sign of the Cross.

Leader: God, our Father, we praise and thank you for being a God who forgives.

All: Amen.

Leader: Jesus, our Savior, we praise and thank you for welcoming sinners and showing us how to live and love.

All: Amen.

Leader: Holy Spirit, giver of God's gifts, we praise and thank you for giving us courage to say "I am sorry" and to forgive others.

All: Amen.

Sing together.

Create in me a clean heart, O God.

A clean heart, O God, create in me.

©Tom Kendzia

✳ People of Faith: A Read Aloud Story

Pope John Paul II   John Paul II was born in Poland. When he was growing up, he saw people who were Christian being unkind to people who were Jewish. Very few people would help the Jews, not even some Church people. This made him sad. Later, when he became pope, John Paul wrote a letter to the people who were Jewish. He said the Church was sorry for the way Christians had treated them. He asked for forgiveness.

Another time, a man shot Pope John Paul II. The pope was hurt and went to the hospital. The police caught the man who had shot the pope and put him in jail. When the pope got better, he went to the jail to meet the man who had shot him. He forgave him. Pope John Paul showed us how to say "I'm sorry" and "I forgive you."

C. 1920–2005

Faith at Home

Faith Focus

- The Eucharist is a sacrament of unity and forgiveness.
- Sin keeps us from being one People of God.
- At Mass we ask God's forgiveness during the Penitential Rite.

Ritual Focus

Penitential Rite The celebration focused on the Penitential Rite. The children prayed the Confiteor. During the week pray the Confiteor with your child.

www.harcourtreligion.com
Visit out Web site for weekly scripture readings and questions, family resources, and more activities.

Act

Share Together Saying "I am sorry" and "I forgive you" are important moments in the life of a family. Asking for and giving forgiveness can strengthen relationships. Sometimes, we seek forgiveness in indirect ways, by doing something special for the person we hurt. Have each family member draw a picture of one way they have seen a family member forgive another. Invite family members to share the story behind the picture.

Pray Together Admitting we have hurt one another and saying "I am sorry" are not always easy things to do. Choose a time to gather for prayer. Open with a prayer to the Holy Spirit. Invite family members to ask for, give, and receive forgiveness for the times they may have hurt one another during the week.

Family Prayer

God of Mercy, thank you for always forgiving us. By the power of the Holy Spirit, help us to change and become more like your Son, Jesus. Make us one in love with you and all the people in our lives. Amen.

31

Faith at Home

Review the five parts of the Faith at Home page with children.

Encourage children:

- to ask family members to review the **Faith Focus** statements
- to share the **Ritual Focus: Penitential Rite** with family members
- to do at least one of the **Act** activities with family members
- to pray the **Family Prayer** with their family at times when the family is together
- to encourage their family members to go to **www.harcourtreligion.com** with them and do the activities for this chapter sometime during the week

Looking Ahead

For Chapter 4, you will need:

- a Bible
- a prayer table
- a candle
- a large glass bowl filled with water
- the *Songs of Celebration* CD
- copies of Activity Master 4 on p. CE9 for each child
- copies of Echo Pantomine 4 on p. CE10

General Instruction of the Roman Missal

"When the Sacred Scriptures are read in the Church, God himself speaks to his people, and Christ, present in his own word, proclaims the Gospel. Therefore, all must listen with reverence to the readings from God's word, for they make up an element of greatest importance in the Liturgy." (no. 29)

Catechism Connection

To deepen your own background and reflection on the word of God, refer to the *Catechism of the Catholic Church,* 101–104, 136, 141, 1154, 1190, 1349, 1408.

Catechist Resources

 Listening to God's Word: Activities and Stories
Eileen Drilling and Judy Rothfork
Liturgy Training Publications

Stories, questions, games, prayers, and blessings for the entire liturgical year

 Threshold to God's Word * (23 min)
Stephen J. Bing
Twenty-Third Publications

How to read the Bible as a basis for prayer

Children's Resources

 The Listening Walk
Paul Showers
Harper Collins

A father and daughter go on a listening walk

 God Speaks to Us in Feeding Stories
(God Speaks to Us Series)
Mary Ann Getty-Sullivan, Marygrace Dulski–Antkowski
Liturgical Press

Scripture stories with meal themes

 * *Available at* **www.harcourtreligion.com**

Catechist Formation

"Your word is a lamp for my feet,
a light for my path."

Psalm 119:105

Feasting on God's Word

Readers of good books know what it means to say a book is "delicious." At times people use the expression, "I devoured that book." In daily life, good books nurture and provide sustenance. They teach lessons. They make other worlds real. So, too, does the Bible.

When one reflects on "feasting" in reference to the Mass, the focus is usually on bread and wine, table and Communion. However, "feasting" at the Eucharist is accomplished from "the one table of God's Word and Christ's Body" (*CCC 103*). Just as readers of good books find nourishment and transformation from their words and stories, so do we, as we listen to the inspired word of God proclaimed and alive in our midst. The breaking open and sharing of God's word is a primary part of our liturgical celebration. Christ, the Word of God, is present in the Scriptures as he is under the appearances of bread and wine which is the Body and Blood of Christ.

Liturgy of the Word

We are called both to listen attentively and to respond to the Scriptures during the Liturgy of the Word. What we see and hear during this part of the Mass is a dialogue between God and his people. Within each of us is another dialogue not necessarily seen or shared with others at the time. It is the internal dialogue inspired by the Holy Spirit that occurs as we listen to God's word. We are inspired by its meaning, and respond to whatever call or challenge we may hear.

When have you experienced the power of God's word in your life?

Which scripture story do you find particularly nurturing or challenging?

Catechist Prayer

Dear God, nourish me with your word. Empower me to be a living witness of your Son, Jesus, in my daily life. Amen.

Lesson Planner

		OBJECTIVES	LESSON PROCESS	ACTIVITIES	MATERIALS
CELEBRATE	10 minutes Pages 32–33	Ritual Focus *Signing* To experience a celebration of the word, including the signing before the proclamation of the Gospel	Celebrate the opening prayer.		**PROGRAM RESOURCES** *Songs of Celebration* CD, track 10 **OTHER MATERIALS** Bible, prayer table, candle, large glass bowl filled with water
	Pages 34–35	To explore the meaning of the ritual action To explain that God is present in the word	Reflect on the celebration. Complete the activity. ✝ Read about and discuss the Sign of the Cross. Describe the Bible as God's word. ✝ Read about and discuss the Bible.	☀ **Reflect** Children reflect on the experience of the celebration and the meaning of signing.	
REMEMBER	30 minutes Pages 36–37	Faith Focus *Why do we listen to God's word?* To explain why it is important to listen to God's word	Discuss why Jesus told stories. 📖 Proclaim the Gospel story. *Matthew 13:1–23* Complete the activity.	☀ **Share** Partners act out scenes from the Gospel story. ◣ **Faith at Home** Suggested activities for the home	**PROGRAM RESOURCES** Copies of Activity Master 4, p. CE9 Copies of Echo Pantomine 4, p. CE10 **OTHER MATERIALS** Lectionary and/or Book of the Gospels
	Pages 38–39	Faith Focus *What happens during the Liturgy of the Word?* To describe the parts of the Liturgy of the Word	Identify the two parts of the Mass. Examine each part of the Liturgy of the Word. ✝ Read about and discuss the readings and the terms ambo, lectionary, Book of the Gospels.	◣ **Faith at Home** Suggested activities for the home	
LIVE	20 minutes Page 40	To encourage children to express how they will listen to and share God's word	Introduce the activity. Pray the Closing Blessing. Read aloud the People of Faith story about Jean Donovan.	☀ **Respond** Children draw ways to share God's word.	**PROGRAM RESOURCES** *Songs of Celebration* CD, track 10
FAITH AT HOME	Page 41	◣ **Faith at Home** To introduce the different parts of the Faith at Home page	Review the Faith at Home page. Encourage children to share this page at home.	☀ **Act** Suggested activities for the home	**PROGRAM RESOURCES** Family Guide, pp. 22–23

CELEBRATE

Objective

To experience a celebration of the word, including Signing before the proclamation of the Gospel

Preparation

Familiarize yourself with the ritual focus for Signing on pages 32–33. You will need:

- a Bible
- a table covered with a white cloth
- a candle and a large glass bowl filled with water on the prayer table

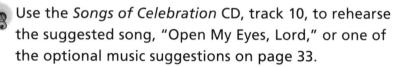 Use the *Songs of Celebration* CD, track 10, to rehearse the suggested song, "Open My Eyes, Lord," or one of the optional music suggestions on page 33.

Select a child to carry the Bible in procession.

We Gather

Invite children to assemble with their books. Gather children into the prayer space with a procession.

- Direct children to follow you and the child carrying the Bible, as you lead the procession.

- As you process, lead children in singing using the *Songs of Celebration* CD, track 10.

- When all are assembled, light the prayer candle.

- Begin prayer, and lead children in the Sign of the Cross.

Follow the order of prayer on pages 32–33.

Chapter **4** We Listen

CELEBRATE

We Gather

Procession

As you sing, walk forward slowly. Follow the person carrying the Bible.

 Sing together.

> Open my ears, Lord.
> Help me to hear your voice.
> Open my eyes, Lord.
> Help me to see.
>
> © 1998 Jesse Manibusan, OCP

Leader: Let us pray.

> Make the Sign of the Cross together.

We Listen

Leader: Father, send the Holy Spirit to open our ears and hearts that we may hear and live your word. We ask this in Jesus' name.

All: Amen.

Leader: A reading from the holy Gospel according to Matthew.

All: Glory to you, Lord.

Ritual Focus: Signing

Leader: Loving Father, we want to live by your word.

> May your word be in our minds.
>
> Trace the Sign of the Cross on your forehead.

32

✺ Liturgical Background

Reverence Reverence is a form of respect given to someone or something that we care deeply about. We reverence the word of God because we believe that God is present in it. During Mass, the Church shows reverence for the word of God by carrying it in procession, incensing it, and bowing before it.

We also show reverence when we:

- listen attentively to the word proclaimed
- apply the word to our own lives
- act on the word

Leader: May your word be on our lips.

Trace the Sign of the Cross on your lips.

May your word be in our hearts.

Trace the Sign of the Cross on your heart.

We ask this through Jesus Christ our Lord.

All: Amen.

Leader: Read Matthew 13:1–23.

The Gospel of the Lord.

All: Praise to you, Lord Jesus Christ.

Sit silently.

We Go Forth

Leader: Loving God, we thank you for your word. Help us remember and share it. We ask this through Jesus Christ our Lord.

All: Amen.

 Sing the opening song together.

33

Ritual Focus: Signing

- Sign yourself reverently and slowly, as you pray the words.

- Allow children time to sign themselves.

We Listen

For the proclamation of the Gospel, you may use a Bible or the adapted reading in the *Child's Book* on pages 36–37.

We Go Forth

Lead the closing prayer. As children process back to their seats, have them sing *Songs of Celebration* CD, track 10, "Open My Eyes, Lord," or one of the optional music suggestions.

Optional Music Suggestions:

"Abre mis ojos" (Open My Eyes) © Jesse Manibusan. Published by OCP

"Jesus, Bread of Life," (refrain) © 2000-Dvorak/ Schaubel, WLP

✦ Ritual Background

Signing The gesture of the signing of forehead, lips, and heart evolved in the ninth through the eleventh centuries, as the Church placed a stronger emphasis on honoring the Gospel. At that time the Signing of the Cross was also done at the close of the Gospel. Its meaning was connected to the scriptural verse about the evil one coming to steal away the word of God from those who did not understand it (*Matthew 13:19*) and the power of the cross to overcome evil.

Other meanings of the signing are:

- a readiness to respond to God's word with courage as expressed in the Letter to the Romans. "For I am not ashamed of the gospel. It is the power of God for the salvation of everyone who believes" (*Romans 1:16*).

- an expression of the assembly's desire to take in the word of God and make it their own.

CELEBRATE

Objective

To explore the meaning of the ritual action of signing before the Gospel

To explain that God is present in the word

Liturgical Catechesis

The purpose of this section is to help children reflect on their experiences of the signs, rituals, prayers, and gestures of the celebration and to lead them to express their own meaning of the experiences. Allow children to share their experiences without commenting on them.

God's Word

- On the board or on chart paper, write the following questions: What did you see? What did you hear? What did you do?

- Guide childen to review the celebration by going over what happened in the prayer.

- Invite children to share their responses to the questions.

- Ask what it was like for them to sign themselves before the Gospel reading.

Reflect

- Invite children to write their responses in the book. Tell children they do not have to complete all three choices.

- Have volunteers share their responses.

The Sign of the Cross

- Read aloud the text.

- Invite children to repeat the signing and the prayer from the opening celebration.

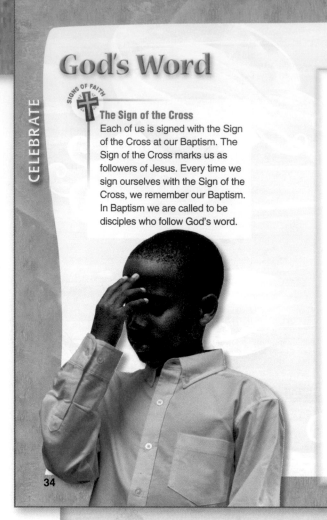

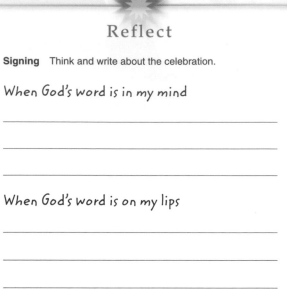

CELEBRATE

God's Word

SIGNS OF FAITH

The Sign of the Cross
Each of us is signed with the Sign of the Cross at our Baptism. The Sign of the Cross marks us as followers of Jesus. Every time we sign ourselves with the Sign of the Cross, we remember our Baptism. In Baptism we are called to be disciples who follow God's word.

34

Reflect

Signing Think and write about the celebration.

When God's word is in my mind

_____

_____

When God's word is on my lips

_____

_____

_____

When God's word is in my heart

_____

_____

✴ Additional Activity

Sing a song Create song lyrics on the board or chart paper:

- List the responses children have shared from their reflection.

- Invite children to add the additional responses.

- Work with children to use their responses to make up a song with gestures.

- Use a familiar tune, such as, "The Farmer in the Dell."

- As a starter line, use the words, "When God's word is in my (mind, lips, heart), I..."

The Bible

We know that the **Bible** is God's own word. Another name used for the Bible is Scriptures. The word *Scriptures* means "writings." God guided humans to write stories of his love and friendship. At Mass we listen to and remember those stories. The good news of the Bible is the same good news that Jesus taught.

God the Father, Jesus, his Son, and the Holy Spirit are with us when we pray for God's word to be in our minds, on our lips, and in our hearts. They help us hear the good news and share it with others.

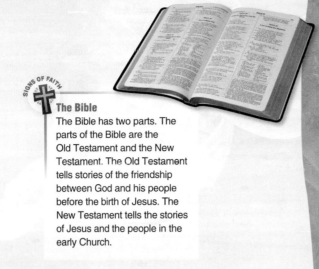

The Bible

The Bible has two parts. The parts of the Bible are the Old Testament and the New Testament. The Old Testament tells stories of the friendship between God and his people before the birth of Jesus. The New Testament tells the stories of Jesus and the people in the early Church.

35

Teaching Tip

Signs of God's presence Bear in mind that sometimes in today's world, children and adults are so busy and easily distracted that they may miss God's word and presence in daily life. Make it a point periodically during the sessions with the children to:

- allow some quiet time to reflect

- pray the prayer, "Let us remember the presence of God"

- point out experiences and events, such as the first sign of spring or the birth of a baby, as signs of God's presence in life today.

The Bible

- Ask children to look at page 35 and find the highlighted word. Bible

- Invite volunteers to share the meaning of the word.

- Ask if anyone can tell the group what is meant by "God's word." Affirm correct responses. Guide responses when needed.

- Read aloud the text.

- Emphasize that when we sign ourselves before the reading of the Gospel, we ask God to be with us.

The Bible

- Invite four children to each read aloud a sentence of the text.

- Do a quick review by asking what the difference is between the Old and New Testaments. Possible responses: The Old Testament is about the time before Jesus; the New Testament is about Jesus; Jesus' stories are in the New Testament but not in the Old Testament.

Objective

To explain why it is important to listen to God's word

Faith Focus

Why do we listen to God's word?
List children's responses on the board or on chart paper.

Hear God's Word

Invite children to look at the scripture illustration. Remind children that it is the Gospel story from the celebration. Ask children to discuss why Jesus told so many stories.

- Summarize the first paragraph. Refer back to children's discussion.

- Write the words *Gospel* and *Good News* on the board or on chart paper, and discuss their definitions.

 Scripture   MATTHEW 13:1–23

The Sower

- Gather children into a story circle or in the prayer space. Remind them that they will be hearing the story from the Gospel of Matthew again.

- Ask what they remember from hearing the Gospel during the celebration.

- Reread the story aloud.

- Or, tell the story using Echo Pantomime 4 on page CE10 of this edition.

Hear God's Word

Faith Focus

Why do we listen to God's word?

Jesus was a storyteller. He told stories about God's love. Sometimes his stories taught a lesson. Jesus wanted people to listen and to understand. Jesus wanted people to share the good news. His stories are in the Gospels. *Gospel* means "good news."

One day Jesus told a story about a sower. A sower is a person who puts seeds on the ground so they can grow.

 Scripture

MATTHEW 13:1–23

The Sower

A sower went out to sow. As he sowed seed, some fell on the edge of the path and the birds ate them. Some fell on rocky ground. There was no soil there and the seed could not take root. The sun came up and burned it. Some seed fell among thorns. The thorns choked the seed and it could not grow. But some seed fell on good soil. These seeds grew and made much fruit.

36

Scripture Background

Parables   This story marks the beginning of a whole section of parables in the Gospel according to Matthew. A parable is a literary form that uses a fictional story to make a point. In the parable of the Sower, Jesus is proclaiming the reign of God and the rich harvest that will be accomplished by the actions of those who hear and understand the word.

There are two possible reasons Jesus spoke in parables:

- Most of the people Jesus taught could not read or write. Using stories was a way to help them remember.

- Many of the parables have surprising endings. Jesus used them to challenge the people to look at beliefs they took for granted.

The people did not understand the story. So Jesus explained it. He said that the seed on the path is like a person who hears God's word but does not understand it. The seed on the rocky ground is like the person who hears God's word but then forgets it. The seed that falls among the thorns is like the person who hears God's word but pays attention to other things and does not follow it. The seed that falls on good soil is like the person who hears God's word, understands it, and follows it.

BASED ON MATTHEW 13:1–23

❷ What lesson did Jesus teach the people in his story?

❷ How do you follow God's word?

Faith at Home

Read the scripture story with your child. Talk about ways you listen to God's word and follow it. Share one of your favorite scripture stories, and talk about what it means to each of you.

Share

Act it out With a partner, choose one of the people Jesus was talking about in the story. Make up that scene from the Gospel story. Act out your part of the story for the rest of the group.

37

✴ Cultural Background

Agriculture Jesus used many agricultural images in his teachings because the majority of the people he taught were members of a peasant society. Agricultural production was the only real source of income. About 90 percent of the people were peasants. The other ten percent would be considered the elite or upper class. This division led to a society in which:

- many of the peasants were exploited through taxation and land rent
- the upper class controlled the economic and religious lives of the peasants
- the good news of Jesus' teachings was a freeing experience for many and an unwelcome challenge for others

---

- Ask children to read silently and identify how many different people Jesus describes in his story. four

❓ Discuss the question. to follow God's word

- Review the images described in the parable.

❓ Discuss the question. List responses on the board or on chart paper. Accept all reasonable responses.

✴ Share

- Organize the group into partners.
- Explain the activity to children.
- Set a time limit.
- Circulate around the pairs to be sure they understand what to do.
- Invite volunteers to act out their parts.

Activity Master

You may wish to use Activity Master 4 on page CE9 to further integrate the meaning of the Gospel story.

▲ Activity Master 4

Review

- *Gospel* means "good news."
- We are called to listen to God's word and follow it.

Objective

To describe the parts of the Liturgy of the Word

Faith Focus

What happens during the Liturgy of the Word?

List children's responses on the board or on chart paper.

The Liturgy of the Word

Ask children to remember the responses they gave on page 34. Explain that during the Liturgy of the Word at Mass, we listen to God's word.

- Invite children to look at the photographs on pages 38 and 39 and tell what they see.

- Summarize the first paragraph on page 38. Emphasize that the Liturgy of the Word is one of two important parts of the Mass, and Jesus is present in God's word.

- Invite children to read the second paragraph to find out how many readings we listen to during the Liturgy of the Word. three

The Readings

- Read aloud the text.

- If you were able to obtain a lectionary or a Book of the Gospels, allow children to look at it.

The Liturgy of the Word

SIGNS OF FAITH

The Readings

The reader reads the first and second readings from a book called the **lectionary**. The lectionary has all the Bible readings for every Sunday in it. The readings are read from a special place called the **ambo**. The Gospel is read from the **Book of the Gospels**, which is carried in procession during the Introductory Rites to show the importance of the four Gospels.

38

Faith Focus

What happens during the Liturgy of the Word?

The Mass has two very important parts. The first part is the **Liturgy of the Word**. The second part is the **Liturgy of the Eucharist**. In the Liturgy of the Word, we celebrate Jesus' presence in the word. In the Liturgy of the Eucharist, we celebrate Jesus' presence when we receive Holy Communion.

During the Liturgy of the Word, we listen to three readings from the Bible. Between the first two readings, we sing or pray a psalm. The psalm is a response, or answer, to God's word.

The first reading is usually from the Old Testament. The second reading is from the part of the New Testament that tells the story of the early followers of Jesus. The third reading is the Gospel. It tells the wonderful good news of Jesus. We greet the Gospel reading with joy. We say or sing "Alleluia!" *Alleluia* means "Praise the Lord."

✳ Catechist Background

Scripture in liturgy The word of God proclaimed in the Liturgy of the Word:

- helps form us into a community

- announces to us the good news of our salvation, beginning in the Old Testament

- teaches us how to live as followers of Jesus and as children of God

- opens us up to listen to God in our everyday lives

Our Response

After the readings, the priest or deacon gives a homily. The homily helps us understand and follow God's word. The homily helps us understand how to live God's word. We respond to God's word when we stand and pray the Creed. We proudly profess what we believe.

Feasting on God's word makes us want to share with others who are hungry for good news. We close the Liturgy of the Word by praying together for the needs of the Church and all people around the world. These special prayers are called the general intercessions or prayer of the faithful.

❷ **What do we call the part of the Mass when we listen to God's word?**

Faith at Home

Talk with your child about how to listen attentively during the Liturgy of the Word. Encourage your child to pay special attention to the readings at Mass this Sunday. Then spend some time after Mass talking about how one of the readings or the homily relates to your family life.

39

Our Response

Explain that during the Liturgy of the Word, we not only listen, but also respond to God's word.

- Summarize the page by writing the terms *homily, the Creed, general intercessions* and *prayers of the faithful* on the board or on chart paper.

- Invite volunteers to read the sentence from the text that describes each term.

- Discuss each of these parts with children.

❷ Invite volunteers to answer the question. the Liturgy of the Word

Review

- The Liturgy of the Word is one of the two important parts of the Mass.

- After we listen to God's word, we pray for the needs of the Church and people around the world.

✸ Sacrament Background

Jewish roots The Liturgy of the Word has its origins in Jewish synagogue worship, which is centered on the word of God in prayers and Scriptures, especially the Torah, the first five books of the Bible. For the Jewish people, the synagogue is both the building itself, and the community of people who assemble to pray, to read the Scriptures, and to hear teachings based on the Scriptures.

During his public life, Jesus went to the synagogue *(Matthew 4:23; Mark 1:21; Luke 4:16–28)* to pray, to teach, and to hear the Scriptures proclaimed. After the Resurrection, the early Church continued to gather to hear the word and break bread together.

Objective

To encourage children to express how they will listen to and share God's word

Share God's Word

Respond

Explain the activity to children. Tell them to include the following in their drawings:

- Who is with them.
- Where they are.
- What is happening.

Closing Blessing

- Gather children into a prayer circle with their books.
- Begin with the Sign of the Cross.
- Read aloud the People of Faith story about Jean Donovan.
  - Pray the prayer.

 End with the *Songs of Celebration* CD, track 10, "Open My Eyes, Lord," or one of the optional music suggestions on page 33.

Share God's Word

Respond

Draw a picture Show how you will share God's word at home or at school.

Closing Blessing

Gather and begin with the Sign of the Cross.

Leader: We praise and thank you, Lord, for the gift of your word.

All: Alleluia.

Leader: Help us to go forth and listen for your word in all we do. Show us how to speak your good news to others.

All: Amen.

Sing together.

Open my ears, Lord.
Help me to hear your voice.
Open my eyes, Lord.
Help me to see.

© 1998 Jesse Manibusan, OCP

40

☀ People of Faith: A Read Aloud Story

Jean Donovan Jean Donovan was a young Catholic American woman who listened to God's word. She showed that God's word was in her heart. She loved people and she loved life. As a college student, Jean began visiting the sick and elderly. She even cooked meals for them. The more she worked with the poor, the more she knew that she did not need a lot of things to make her happy. She could be happy by serving others. Later, Jean became a missionary in Central America and gave up her life for her faith.

C. 1953–1980

Faith at Home

Faith Focus

- The Bible is God's word written in human words.

- We listen to the word of God during the Liturgy of the Word.

- When we listen to God's word, we want to share it with others.

Ritual Focus

Signing The celebration focused on listening to God's word. The children prayed by signing themselves with the Sign of the Cross on their forehead, lips, and heart. They prayed that God's word would be with them. At appropriate times during the week, pray the signing prayer on pages 32–33 with your child.

www.harcourtreligion.com
Visit our Web site for weekly scripture readings and questions, family resources, and more activities.

Act

Share Together Using newspapers and magazines, cut out stories and pictures that show that God's word is alive today in people and events. Name some people who are in need of seeing God's word alive today. Create a family prayer of the faithful, and pray it this week during times you are together.

Do Together Read Matthew 13:1–23, and talk about the question, "How can we bring the word of God to someone in need this week?" Check your parish bulletin for the names of those who might appreciate a get-well card or a card of encouragement. Have family members include their favorite verses.

Family Prayer

Jesus, bless us as we listen for your word this week. Open our eyes, our hearts, and minds that we will become more faithful followers and have the courage to spread your word to all those we meet. Amen.

41

Faith at Home

Review the five parts of the Faith at Home page with children.

Encourage children:

- to ask family members to review the **Faith Focus** statements

- to share the **Ritual Focus: Signing** with family members

- to do at least one of the **Act** activities with family members

- to pray the **Family Prayer** with their family at times when the family is together

- to encourage their family members to go to **www.harcourtreligion.com** with them and do the activities for this chapter sometime during the week

Looking Ahead

For Chapter 5, you will need:

- a Bible

- a prayer table

- a candle

- a large glass bowl filled with water

- the *Songs of Celebration* CD

- copies of Activity Master 5 on p. CE11 for each child

- copies of Scripture Narration 5 on p. CE12 for participants

General Instruction of the Roman Missal

"...Even though the faithful no longer bring from their own possessions the bread and wine intended for the liturgy...the rite of carrying up the offerings still retains its force and its spiritual significance.

"It is well also that money or other gifts for the poor or for the Church, brought by the faithful or collected in the church, should be received...." (no. 73)

Catechism Connection

To deepen your own background and reflection on the signs of bread and wine, refer to the *Catechism of the Catholic Church, 1333–1136*.

Catechist Resources

 "The Roman Catholic Mass Today" *(30 min)*
Liturgy Training Publications
Focuses on the major movements of the Mass

 The Bread of God: Nurturing a Eucharistic Imagination
Tony Kelly C.Ss.R.
Liguori Publications
Examines a way of thinking that helps integrate the Eucharist into daily living

Children's Resources

 Tomie DePaola's Book of Bible Stories: New International Version
Tomie DePaola
Puffin
Retells favorite stories from the Old and New Testaments

 A Child's View of Community *(10 min)*
St. Anthony Messenger Press, Catholic Update Video
Invites children and adults to see the workings of the Holy Spirit in their lives

 * *Available at* **www.harcourtreligion.com**

Catechist Formation

> "This is my body, which will be given for you; ..."
>
> Luke 22:19

Preparing Through Thanksgiving

Many families begin their meals together by praying the grace before meals in which they give thanks to God for the gifts they will be sharing at the table. In the same way, as Catholics prepare to celebrate the Liturgy of the Eucharist, they give thanks to God for the gifts they have, especially the bread and wine, which will become their spiritual food and drink.

Through the power of the Holy Spirit and the words and actions of the priest, this bread and wine will become the Body and Blood of Christ. Those gathered at Mass recognize that after the consecration, Christ is present under the appearances of bread and wine. As the community celebrates the sacramental presence of Christ, it also celebrates the sacrifice that Christ made on behalf of all through his suffering and death on the cross.

The Cross

Because the Mass is a re–presentation of Jesus' sacrifice on the cross, the cross always has a prominent place near the altar. Frequently, it is carried in procession so that the assembly will remember they are also making the journey toward Jerusalem, where Jesus was put to death. The preparation for the Eucharist reminds the assembly that they, too, are called to share in Christ's sacrifice through their service to one another (*John 13:1–16*).

What role does the cross have in your life?

What ways do you share in Christ's sacrifice by living on behalf of others?

Catechist Prayer

Help me, Holy Spirit, to take up the cross of Jesus Christ with courage. May the power of his sacrifice guide me in serving others. Amen.

Lesson Planner

		OBJECTIVES	LESSON PROCESS	ACTIVITIES	MATERIALS
CELEBRATE	15 minutes Pages 42–43	Ritual Focus *Honoring the Cross* To experience a celebration of the word, including Honoring the Cross	Celebrate the opening prayer.		PROGRAM RESOURCES *Songs of Celebration* CD, track 11 OTHER MATERIALS Bible, cross or crucifix, prayer table, candle, large bowl filled with water
	Pages 44–45	To explore the meaning of the ritual action To teach the meaning of sacrifice	Reflect on the celebration. Complete the activity. Read about and discuss the meaning of the cross or crucifix. Discuss sacrifice. Read about and discuss the altar.	**Reflect** Children reflect on the experience of the celebration and the meaning of Honoring the Cross.	
REMEMBER	30 minutes Pages 46–47	Faith Focus *What does Jesus tell us about serving others?* To explain that Jesus wants us to serve others	Discuss what Jesus tells us about serving others. Proclaim the Gospel story. *John 13:1–16* Complete the activity.	**Share** Children write a story about a sacrifice. **Faith at Home** Suggested activities for the home	PROGRAM RESOURCES Copies of Activity Master 5, p. CE11 Copies of Scripture Narration 5, p. CE12 OTHER MATERIALS Props for dramatizing the Gospel story
	Pages 48–49	Faith Focus *What gifts do we bring to the altar?* To explain why we present gifts at Mass	Explain that the Preparation of the Gifts is part of the Liturgy of the Eucharist. Read about the bread and wine used as food for souls.	**Faith at Home** Suggested activities for the home	
LIVE	15 minutes Page 50	To encourage children to serve others and praise God	Introduce the activity. Pray the Closing Blessing. Read aloud the People of Faith story about Saint Maximilian Kolbe.	**Respond** Children discuss ways of serving and color the cross.	PROGRAM RESOURCES *Songs of Celebration* CD, track 11
FAITH AT HOME	Page 51	**Faith at Home** To introduce the different parts of the Faith at Home page	Review the Faith at Home page. Encourage children to share this page at home.	**Act** Suggested activities for the home	PROGRAM RESOURCES Family Guide, pp. 24–25

CELEBRATE

Objective

To experience a celebration of the word, including a ritual of Honoring the Cross

Preparation

Familiarize yourself with the movements of the ritual focus for Honoring the Cross on pages 42–43.

Prepare the prayer space ahead of time. You will need:

- a Bible
- a table covered with a white cloth
- a cross or crucifix
- a candle and a large glass bowl filled with water on the prayer table

Prepare the children ahead of time for the ritual of Honoring the Cross. Explain that they may touch the cross or bow before it at the appropriate time.

Use the *Songs of Celebration* CD, track 11, to rehearse the suggested song, "We Praise You" or one of the optional music suggestions on page 43.

Select children to carry the cross and the Bible in procession.

We Gather

Invite children to assemble with their books. Gather children into the prayer space with a procession.

- Direct children to follow you and the child carrying the Bible, as you lead the procession.
- As you process, lead children in singing using the *Songs of Celebration* CD, track 11.
- When all are assembled, light the prayer candle.
- Begin prayer, and lead the children in the Sign of the Cross.

Follow the order of prayer on pages 42–43.

We Gather

Procession

As you sing, walk forward slowly. Follow the person carrying the cross and Bible.

🎵 Sing together.

> We praise you, O Lord
> For all your works are wonderful.
> We praise you, O Lord
> Forever is your love.
>
> © 1978 Damean Music

Leader: Let us pray.

> Make the Sign of the Cross together.

Ritual Focus: Honoring the Cross

Leader: God gives us many gifts. He gives us sun and rain. He gives us family and friends. He gives us our life. The most important gift God gives us is his Son, Jesus. Jesus shows us how to live. When Jesus died on the cross, he gave his life for all people. Let us think about what a wonderful gift Jesus gave us.

Sit silently.

Come forward, and put your hand on the cross.

42

✷ Liturgical Background

The cross The practice of venerating, or honoring, the cross during the liturgy of Good Friday comes from the fourth century in Jerusalem, where people venerated a relic of the true cross.

- Today we use a representation of the cross for veneration. It must be made of wood, to recall the actual material used in the crucifixion.

- There is no veneration of the cross at Sunday Mass, but the gesture might be used in a penitential service, for example, to increase awareness of Christ's sacrifice for our sins.

- A depiction of Christ crucified is present in every Catholic church. Spiritual devotion to the suffering Messiah has long been a strong element of Catholic piety.

We Listen

Leader: Gracious God, open our hearts to hear your word. We ask this through Jesus Christ our Lord.

All: Amen.

Leader: A reading from the holy Gospel according to John.

All: Glory to you, Lord.

Trace the Sign of the Cross on your forehead, lips, and heart.

Leader: Read John 13:1–16.

The Gospel of the Lord.

All: Praise to you, Lord Jesus Christ.

Sit silently.

Leader: Lord God, send us the Holy Spirit to show us how to live for others. We ask this in the name of Jesus, your Son.

All: Amen.

Leader: Let us pray as Jesus taught us:

Pray the Lord's Prayer together.

Let us offer each other the Sign of Peace.

Offer one another a sign of Christ's peace. Say: "The Peace of the Lord be with you." Answer: "And also with you."

We Go Forth

Leader: Loving God, send us out to share our lives with others. We ask this through Jesus Christ our Lord.

All: Amen.

 Sing the opening song together.

43

Ritual Focus: Honoring the Cross

- Direct the children to come forward one by one.

- You may wish to play the *Songs of Celebration* CD, track 11, as background music during the ritual.

We Listen

For the proclamation of the Gospel, you may use a Bible or the adapted reading in the *Child's Book* on pages 46–47.

- Invite children to stand for the Lord's Prayer and the Sign of Peace. You may want to refer children to page 96 of their books for the words to the Lord's Prayer.

We Go Forth

- Lead the closing prayer. Have children return to their seats. As children process back to their seats, have them sing *Songs of Celebration* CD, track 11, "We Praise You," or one of the optional music suggestions.

 Optional Music Suggestions:

"Demos gracias al Señor," © Al Valverde. Published by OCP

"Give Thanks and Remember," Jack Miffleton, © 1975 WLP

Objective

To explore the meaning of the ritual action of Honoring the Cross

To teach the meaning of sacrifice

Liturgical Catechesis

The purpose of this section is to help children reflect on their experiences of the signs, rituals, prayers, and gestures of the celebration and to lead them to express their own meaning of the experiences. Allow children to share their experiences without commenting on them.

The Cross

- On the board or on chart paper, write the following questions: What did you see? What did you hear? What did you do?

- Guide children to review the celebration by reviewing what happened in the prayer.

- Invite children to share their responses to the questions.

Reflect

- Ask children to write their responses in the book. Tell children they do not have to complete all three choices.

- Have volunteers share their responses.

The Cross

- Invite children to look at and touch the cross or crucifix used in the celebration.

- Read the text aloud.

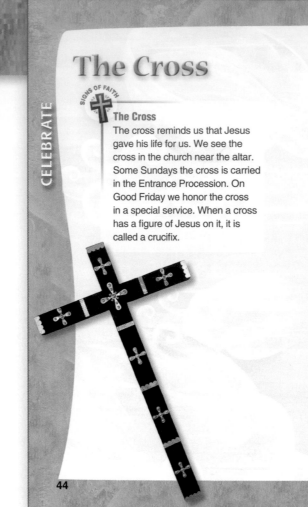

The Cross

SIGNS OF FAITH

The Cross

The cross reminds us that Jesus gave his life for us. We see the cross in the church near the altar. Some Sundays the cross is carried in the Entrance Procession. On Good Friday we honor the cross in a special service. When a cross has a figure of Jesus on it, it is called a crucifix.

CELEBRATE

44

Reflect

Honoring the Cross   Think and write about the celebration.

When I think about all of God's gifts

_____

_____

When I put my hand on the cross

_____

_____

When I think about Jesus

_____

_____

Additional Activity

Make crosses   Have each child make a cross to take home and hang in a place where it can be seen every day.

- Have available paper, markers, scissors, yarn, glue, and any other safe and tactile supplies that children might use to make their crosses. Be sure the paper is sturdy enough to sustain the trip home.

- Distribute the basic art supplies of paper and markers.

- Show children where they can get more decorations for their crosses. Have a table set apart with the additional tactile supplies.

- Tell children to make a special cross that will remind them each time they look at it how much Jesus loves them.

- As children finish, display the completed crosses.

- At the end of the session, invite children to take their crosses home.

Sacrifice

The cross reminds us that Jesus died for us. He died for our sins. He gave up his life as a sacrifice for all people. To *sacrifice* means to "give up something out of love for someone else." What a wonderful gift Jesus gave us—his life.

We sacrifice when we share with others. When we give up something to help someone, we sacrifice. We sacrifice out of love.

When the Church gathers for Mass, we remember the sacrifice of Jesus on the cross. The Mass is our sacrifice, too. At Mass we remember what we have done for God and others. We give God the gift of our lives.

The Altar

The **altar** is the central table in the front of the church. It is a sign of Jesus' presence with us. It is also a sign that the Mass is a sacrifice and a meal. Another name for the altar is "the Table of the Lord."

45

Sacrifice

- Read aloud the first two paragraphs.
- Ask children to think about a time when they made a sacrifice for someone else.
- Invite children to share their stories with a partner.
- When they have finished sharing, ask them why they made the sacrifice and how it felt to sacrifice.
- Summarize the last paragraph.

The Altar

- Invite children to read the text silently and find one thing the altar is a sign of. Jesus' presence; Mass is a sacrifice and a meal.
- Have children look at the picture of the altar on page 82 of the Words of Faith glossary.

Teaching Tip

Altar   One of the meanings of the word *altar* is "place of sacrifice." In Hebrew the root of that word means, "to slaughter and cut up for the purpose of sacrifice."

Altars actually go back to pre-biblical times, when people slaughtered animals as a sacrifice to the gods and then placed the animals on the altar, either to be left there or to be burned.

Sacrifice has always been part of human worship.

- We believe Jesus' death on the cross was the ultimate sacrifice.
- The Mass is the ultimate sacrifice.
- We participate in that sacrifice as we bring the gift of our lives to the altar.

Objective

To explain that Jesus wants us to serve others

Faith Focus

What does Jesus tell us about serving others?
List children's responses on the board or on chart paper.

We Serve Others

Recall with children the arrival of Jesus in Jerusalem on Palm Sunday. Tell them that this chapter's scripture story takes place a few days later, on the first Holy Thursday.

- Ask children to describe what is happening in the illustration. *Jesus is washing his Apostles' feet.*

- Read the text aloud.

 Scripture   JOHN 13:1–16

The Washing of the Feet

- Gather children into a story circle or in the prayer space. Remind them that they will be hearing the story from the Gospel of John again.

- Ask what they remember from hearing the Gospel during the celebration.

- Reread the story aloud.

- Or, select some children to narrate the story. Use the text on page CE12 of this edition.

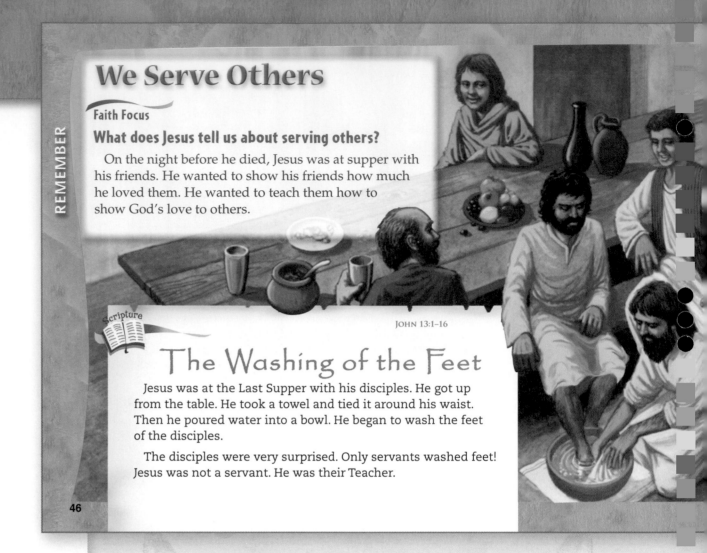

We Serve Others

Faith Focus

What does Jesus tell us about serving others?

On the night before he died, Jesus was at supper with his friends. He wanted to show his friends how much he loved them. He wanted to teach them how to show God's love to others.

JOHN 13:1–16

The Washing of the Feet

Jesus was at the Last Supper with his disciples. He got up from the table. He took a towel and tied it around his waist. Then he poured water into a bowl. He began to wash the feet of the disciples.

The disciples were very surprised. Only servants washed feet! Jesus was not a servant. He was their Teacher.

46

📖 Scripture Background

The Gospel of John   John's Gospel has a long account of the Last Supper but does not describe the institution of the Eucharist. Instead, this gospel describes Jesus' arising from supper and taking a basin and towel to wash the feet of his disciples. Afterward, Jesus interprets this action, explaining, "I have given you a model to follow" *(John 13:15)*.

The washing of feet stresses the service dimension of following Jesus. It presents Jesus, the Master, performing an act usually done either by the lowest servant in the household or by the host himself as a symbol of respect for his guests. The Gospel of John emphasizes that all those who follow Jesus and who are "washed clean" are one with him. Disciples are recognized by their imitation of Jesus.

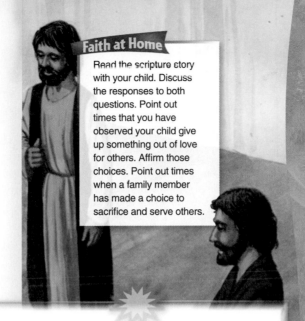

Peter said to Jesus, "You will never wash my feet." Jesus said, "If you do not let me wash your feet, you cannot be my friend." Then Jesus washed the feet of all the disciples.

When he was finished, Jesus said, "Do you understand what I just did? You call me 'teacher' and 'master.' I am. If I have washed your feet, then you should wash one another's feet. What I do for you, you should do for others."

BASED ON JOHN 13:1–16

❓ Why do you think Jesus washed his friends' feet?

❓ What does Jesus want you to do for others?

Faith at Home

Read the scripture story with your child. Discuss the responses to both questions. Point out times that you have observed your child give up something out of love for others. Affirm those choices. Point out times when a family member has made a choice to sacrifice and serve others.

Share

Write a story On a separate sheet of paper, make up a story about a child your age who makes a sacrifice for a brother, a sister, or a friend.

47

- Read the two questions to children.
- Organize children into groups of three or four. Invite them to share in their groups as many answers to the questions as they can in one minute.
- Have volunteers share responses from their group.

❓ **What does Jesus want you to do for others?** Possible responses: be kind, share, serve others, make sacrifices for others

❓ **Why do you think Jesus washed his friends' feet?** Their feet were dirty; he wanted to show he loved them; he wanted to serve them.

Share

- Organize children into pairs to plan their stories. Explain that children are to write a story with their partner about a sacrifice. Set a time limit.
- Have children share their work with the class.

Activity Master

You may wish to use Activity Master 5 on page CE11 to further integrate the meaning of the Gospel story.

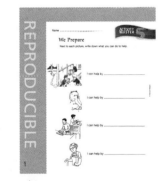

▲ Activity Master 5

Review

- Jesus taught that we should show God's love to others.
- We show love for others by serving them.

Travel in Jesus' time Travel was very difficult in the first century. Roads were not paved. People went about barefoot or in sandals. Some homes were equipped with a small but welcoming place for people to wash and refresh their feet. In this place there was a stationary tub with still or "running" water as in a fountain. In a modest home, foot washing might be accomplished using a basin and towels. Often travelers washed their own feet upon arrival. However, if there were servants in the household, they would perform the task for invited guests. When a guest was to be honored on a special occasion, the host himself might offer this service as a sign of respect.

Objective

To explain why we present gifts at Mass

Faith Focus

What gifts do we bring to the altar?

List children's responses on the board or on chart paper.

The Sacrifice of the Mass

Write the terms *Liturgy of the Eucharist, Preparation of the Altar and Gifts,* and *sacrifice* on the board or on chart paper. Explain the terms as you work through the text.

- Recall the meaning of the washing of the feet.

- Summarize the information in the first paragraph of text.

- Point out that every Mass makes present again Jesus' sacrifice.

- Read aloud the rest of the text.

Bread and Wine

- Refer to the Words of Faith glossary on pages 82–87.

- Discuss how bread and wine are not just food for our bodies, but are food for our souls, when the bread and wine become the Body and Blood of Jesus during Mass.

The Sacrifice of the Mass

REMEMBER

SIGNS OF FAITH

Bread and Wine

Bread and wine are foods that people use for special meals. At Mass we use bread that is made without yeast. The wine comes from grapes. By the power of the Holy Spirit and the words and actions of the priest, the bread and wine become the Body and Blood of Jesus. They become our spiritual food.

Faith Focus

What gifts do we bring to the altar?

When Jesus washed the feet of the disciples, he showed us how to give our lives for others. Jesus gave his life for us on the cross. He saved us from our sins by his life, his death, and his Resurrection.

At Mass we remember Jesus' sacrifice during the Liturgy of the Eucharist. *Eucharist* means "thanksgiving." The Liturgy of the Eucharist is the second main part of the Mass. Through the power of the Holy Spirit and the words and actions of the priest, Jesus offers again the gift of himself to his Father.

During the Liturgy of the Eucharist, we thank God the Father for Jesus' sacrifice on the cross. We bring our lives and our sacrifices to the altar.

The sacrifices we make during the week are our gifts to God. They prepare us to join in Jesus' sacrifice.

48

 ## Catechist Background

The gifts   As early as the second century, the people began to bring material gifts to the Eucharist for the needs of the Church or for the poor. The offering of these gifts was gradually included in the celebration of the Mass.

Often the gifts included the bread and wine for the celebration. The people brought the gifts to the altar, and the priest received them as an offering.

In the Roman liturgy of the seventh century, the gifts—mostly bread and wine—were not brought directly to the altar by the people but were collected by the celebrant and his assistants after the Gospel reading. When more was collected than was necessary for the Mass, only what was needed for Mass was placed on the altar. The rest was put on special tables and later given to the clergy and the poor.

Preparation of the Gifts

The Liturgy of the Eucharist begins with the Preparation of the Altar and the Gifts. Members of the assembly bring the bread and wine to the priest and they are placed on the altar.

We also offer gifts of money or other gifts. This offering is called a **collection**. These offerings help the parish do its work and take care of those in need. They are also a sign of our sacrifice.

The priest prepares the bread and wine and gives God thanks for his goodness.

We answer, "Blessed be God forever."

Then the priest prays that our sacrifice be acceptable to God.

We answer, "May the Lord accept the sacrifice at your hands for the praise and glory of his name, for our good, and the good of all his Church."

❷ What gifts do you bring to Mass?

Faith at Home

Discuss your child's response to the question. Talk about the purpose of the collection. Point out ways your child can contribute his or her time, talent, or money as a gift to God. Use this page to review the responses for the Preparation of the Gifts.

49

Teaching Tip

Bring yourselves Children at this age can be particularly sensitive to what they perceive is expected of them and their families. Assure the children that the collection is only one way of sharing our gifts with our parish family. Contributing to the collection is not a requirement for attending Mass. This should alleviate anxiety for those children who cannot or whose families cannot contribute very much financially to the parish.

Preparation of the Gifts

Recall with children that members of the assembly often carry up the gifts at Saturday evening and Sunday Masses. Have children who have carried up the gifts share the experience.

- Use the Teaching Tip below to help discuss the types of gifts that are collected at Mass.

- Ask children to read the text silently and tell what the parish does with collection offerings. The parish uses them to support the parish and take care of needy people.

- Finish reading the text aloud. Invite children to repeat the Mass responses after you.

❷ Discuss the question to help children reflect on their part in the Preparation of the Gifts. Possible responses: money, my sacrifices, my prayers, my actions

Review

- The Liturgy of the Eucharist is the second main part of the Mass.

- During the Preparation of the Gifts, we offer ourselves and our gifts to help others.

Objective

To encourage children to serve others and praise God

I Serve Others

Respond

Explain the activity to children. Help them brainstorm ways that they can serve others during the week. They can include ways of serving:

- at home
- at school
- in church

Closing Blessing

- Gather children into a prayer circle with their books.
- Begin with the Sign of the Cross.
- Read aloud the People of Faith story about Saint Maximilian Kolbe.
- Pray the prayer.

 End by leading children in singing *Songs of Celebration* CD, track 11, "We Praise You," or one of the optional music suggestions on page 43.

I Serve Others

Respond

Color the cross In the spaces around the cross, write ways that you will serve others this week. Then color the cross.

Closing Blessing

Gather and begin with the Sign of the Cross.

Leader: God, our Father, we praise and thank you for the gift of your Son, Jesus.

All: Amen.

Leader: Jesus, our Savior, we praise and thank you for giving up your life for us.

All: Amen.

Sing together.

We praise you, O Lord,
For all your works are wonderful.
We praise you, O Lord,
Forever is your love.

© 1978 Damean Music

☀ People of Faith: A Read Aloud Story

Saint Maximilian Kolbe

Maximilian Kolbe was born in Poland. He was considered a "wild young boy." He was very smart and loved science and mathematics. Some people thought he would become a scientist, but he became a Franciscan priest. During World War II, Maximilian was a prisoner in a Nazi concentration camp. One of his fellow prisoners was condemned to die. The man begged the Nazis for his life. He wanted to be able to take care of his family after the war. Maximilian offered to take his place. When Pope John Paul II made Maximilian a saint, the man whose life he had saved was at the ceremony.

C. 1894–1941

Faith at Home

Faith Focus
- Jesus sacrificed his life for us when he died on the cross.
- The Mass is a sacrifice.
- At Mass, through the power of the Holy Spirit and the words and actions of the priest, Jesus offers again the gift of himself to his Father.

Ritual Focus
Honoring the Cross The celebration focused on Honoring the Cross. The children reverenced the cross. Place a cross or crucifix in a place where the family gathers and says evening prayers.

www.harcourtreligion.com
Visit our Web site for weekly scripture readings and questions, family resources, and more activities.

Act

Share Together Read John 13:1–16. Talk about what Jesus meant when he said, "What I do for you, you should do for others." Make a list of people who serve your family, such as sanitation workers, street crossing guards, doctors, or dentists. Discuss ways your family can thank these people for sharing their gifts.

Do Together As a family, name some neighbors, family members, or friends who are in need of help or companionship, such as someone who is sick, lives alone, or needs to be tutored. Make a list of actions your family can take to serve these people sometime in the next month. Decide who will do what, and then mark it on the calendar.

Family Prayer
Gracious God, thank you for the gift of each other and especially for the gift of Jesus. Help us remain in your love and teach us to share it with others. Amen.

51

Faith at Home

Review the five parts of the Faith at Home page with children.

Encourage children:

- to ask family members to review the Faith Focus statements
- to share the **Ritual Focus: Honoring the Cross** with family members
- to do at least one of the 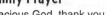 Act activities with family members
- to pray the **Family Prayer** with their family at times when the family is together
- to encourage their family members to go to **www.harcourtreligion.com** with them and do the activities for this chapter sometime during the week

Looking Ahead

For Chapter 6, you will need:

- a Bible
- a prayer table
- a candle
- a large glass bowl filled with water
- the *Songs of Celebration* CD
- copies of Activity Master 6 on p. CE13 for each child
- copies of the Scripture Drama 6 on pp. CE14–15 for participants

General Instruction of the Roman Missal

"Now the center and summit of the entire celebration begins: namely, the Eucharistic Prayer, that is, the prayer of thanksgiving and sanctification…. The meaning of the Prayer is that the entire congregation of the faithful should join itself with Christ in confessing the great deeds of God and in the offering of Sacrifice. The Eucharistic Prayer demands that all listen to it with reverence and in silence." (no. 78)

Catechism Connection

To deepen your own background and reflection on the Eucharist as a memorial, refer to the *Catechism of the Catholic Church, 1362–1366.*

Catechist Resources

 This Sacred Meal: The Eucharist in Our Lives *(21 min)*
Twenty-Third Publications
Explores the Eucharist from an adult perspective

 The Truth About the Eucharist
Father John Dowling
Liguori
Explains the doctrine of the Real Presence of Christ in the Eucharist

Children's Resources

 Close Encounters with the Mass* *(14 min)*
Oblate Media and Communication
Explores the Eucharist as a celebration of a meal, as a thanksgiving, and as a sacrifice

 God Speaks to Us in Feeding Stories*
Mary Ann Getty-Sullivan, Marygrace Dulski–Antkowski
Liturgical Press
Beautifully illustrated adapted Bible stories about meals that show God's continuing care for his people

 * *Available at* **www.harcourtreligion.com**

Catechist Formation

> "They ate their meals with exultation and sincerity of heart, praising God and enjoying favor with all the people."
>
> Acts of the Apostles 2:46–47

Remembering and Presence

We often recall people who have died or who live far away. We have a sense of their presence. During the Eucharist we do more than remember or recall the person of Jesus or the events of salvation history. In the Eucharistic Prayer we have more than a sense of the presence of the Risen Lord. He is there as the eternal high priest, offering the Eucharistic sacrifice through the ministry of the priests and under the appearances of bread and wine.

During the Eucharistic prayer of the Mass, the assembly hears and participates in the story of God's presence throughout all of human history, especially through the death and Resurrection of Christ, and recognizes God's continuing presence. "In the sense of Sacred Scripture the *memorial* is not merely the recollection of the past events but the proclamation of the mighty works wrought by God for men. In the liturgical celebration of these events, they become in a certain way present and real." *(Catechism of the Catholic Church, 1363)*

Joined with All Creation

Through prayer and song, the community is joined with all creation, both living and dead, because the death and Resurrection of Christ has created an unbreakable bond between heaven and earth. The Eucharistic Prayer opens by recounting God's creation and the ways in which God's faithfulness has been revealed throughout salvation history. The center point of the Eucharistic Prayer is the institution narrative and the consecration. It concludes by remembering all people, including those who have died. The Amen that the community proclaims at the end of the prayer is a sign of its communion in giving glory, honor, and thanksgiving to God for what he has done.

Which part of the Eucharistic Prayer seems to draw your attention each week?

When you say or sing the Amen, what images does it bring to mind? What images does the Eucharistic Prayer bring to mind?

Catechist Prayer

Blessed are you, O God of all creation. May my life reflect the glory of your love in all that I say and do. Amen.

Lesson Planner

		OBJECTIVES	LESSON PROCESS	ACTIVITIES	MATERIALS
CELEBRATE	15 minutes Pages 52–53	Ritual Focus *Memorial Acclamation* To experience a celebration of the word, including the gesture of kneeling and the Memorial Acclamation	Celebrate the opening prayer.		PROGRAM RESOURCES *Songs of Celebration* CD, track 12 OTHER MATERIALS Bible, prayer table, candle, large glass bowl filled with water
	Pages 54–55	To explore the meaning of the ritual action To explain the meaning of the Eucharistic Prayer	Reflect on the celebration. Complete the activity. Read about and discuss kneeling. Explore the mystery of the Eucharistic Prayer. Read about and discuss the role of the priest.	**Reflect** Children reflect on the experience of the celebration and the meaning of Christ's presence.	
REMEMBER	30 minutes Pages 56–57	Faith Focus *What does Jesus tell his friends?* To explain the significance of the Last Supper	Discuss the importance of the Last Supper. Proclaim the Gospel story. *Matthew 26:26–28; Luke 22:14–20* Complete the activity.	**Share** Children complete phrases from the Last Supper story. **Faith at Home** Suggested activities for the home	PROGRAM RESOURCES Copies of Activity Master 6, p. CE13 Copies of Scripture Drama 6, pp. CE14–15
	Pages 58–59	Faith Focus *What do we remember and give thanks for during the Eucharistic Prayer?* To describe the Consecration, Memorial Acclamation, and Great Amen	Relate the Consecration, Memorial Acclamation, and Great Amen to the Last Supper. Read about the Blessed Sacrament and discuss why the tabernacle is important.	**Faith at Home** Suggested activities for the home	
LIVE	15 minutes Page 60	To help children remember and give thanks for gifts from God	Introduce the activity. Pray the Closing Blessing. Read aloud the People of Faith story about Paschal Baylon.	**Respond** Children color a stained glass window picture.	PROGRAM RESOURCES *Songs of Celebration* CD, track 12
FAITH AT HOME	Page 61	**Faith at Home** To introduce the different parts of the Faith at Home page	Review the Faith at Home page. Encourage children to share this page at home.	**Act** Suggested activities for the home	PROGRAM RESOURCES Family Guide, pp. 26–27

CELEBRATE

Objective

To experience a celebration of the word, including the gesture of kneeling and the Memorial Acclamation

Preparation

Familiarize yourself with the movements of the ritual focus for Memorial Acclamation on pages 52–53.

Prepare the prayer space ahead of time. You will need:

- a Bible
- a table covered with a white cloth
- a candle and a large glass bowl filled with water on the prayer table

 Use the *Songs of Celebration* CD, track 12, to rehearse the suggested song, "Te alabaré, Señor," or one of the optional music suggestions on page 53.

Select a child to carry the Bible in procession.

We Gather

- Invite children to assemble with their books.
- Gather children into the prayer space with a procession.

 As you process, lead children in singing using the *Songs of Celebration* CD, track 12.

- When all are assembled, light the prayer candle.
- Begin prayer, and lead the children in the Sign of the Cross.

Follow the order of prayer on pages 52–53.

We Listen

For the proclamation of the Gospel, you may use a Bible or the adapted reading in the *Child's Book* on pages 56–57.

We Gather

Procession

As you sing, walk forward slowly. Follow the person carrying the Bible.

Te alabaré, Señor; tú me has librado.

I will praise you Lord; you have rescued me.

Tony Alonso © 2003 GIA Pub, Inc.

Leader: Let us pray.

Make the Sign of the Cross together.

We Listen

Leader: Loving Father, we come before you to remember and give thanks for your Son, Jesus. Open our hearts to the Holy Spirit to understand your word. We ask this through Jesus Christ our Lord.

All: Amen.

Leader: A reading from the holy Gospel according to Luke.

All: Glory to you, Lord.

Trace the Sign of the Cross on your forehead, lips, and heart.

Leader: Read Luke 22:14–20.

The Gospel of the Lord.

All: Praise to you, Lord Jesus Christ.

Sit silently.

52

✦ Liturgical Background

Kneeling Kneeling can be a sign of penitence, humility, and submission. It is also a posture of prayer, adoration, and reverence. When we kneel during the Eucharistic Prayer at Mass, we express reverence.

Throughout the worldwide Church, kneeling to show reverence for the presence of Christ in the sacrament of his Body and Blood, is the posture recommended at the consecration.

In the dioceses of the United States, however, the people kneel during the whole Eucharistic Prayer, unless some good reason prevents it. Those who do not kneel make a profound bow when the priest genuflects after the consecration *(GIRM 43)*.

Leader: Every time we gather together at the Eucharist, we know Jesus comes again to be with us. We are happy. We give God the Father thanks and praise for the mystery of Jesus' presence. We pray.

Kneel.

Let us proclaim the mystery of faith:

All: Christ has died.

Christ is risen.

Christ will come again.

Stand.

Leader: Let us pray as Jesus taught us:

Pray the Lord's Prayer together.

Leader: Let us offer each other the Sign of Peace.

Offer one another a sign of Christ's peace.
Say: "The Peace of the Lord be with you."
Answer: "And also with you."

We Go Forth

Leader: Loving Father, send us forth to bring Jesus' presence to one another. Help us to remember him. We ask this through Jesus Christ our Lord.

All: Amen.

Sing the opening song together.

53

Ritual Background

Memorial Acclamation Memory is important to liturgy. When we remember the death and Resurrection of Jesus in the liturgy, we do more than just acknowledge something that happened long ago. We affirm that this sacred event is present to us right now through the words and actions of the priest and the working of the Holy Spirit.

When the liturgy was reformed after the Second Vatican Council, an acclamation was inserted after the consecration. This acclamation begins by proclaiming the "mystery of faith," reflecting the ancient Latin expression *Mysterium fidei,* which means "the mystery of faith." It is called a Memorial Acclamation and is located in the heart of the Eucharistic Prayer, the whole of which recalls the death and Resurrection of Jesus. The Memorial Acclamation expresses the assembly's faith in the Paschal mystery.

Ritual Focus: Memorial Acclamation

- Direct children to kneel and stand at appropriate times.

- You may wish to sing the Memorial Acclamation. If so, use a tune that is often sung in your parish.

- You may want to refer children to page 96 in their books for the words of the Lord's Prayer.

- If children can say the Lord's Prayer without their books, invite them to extend their arms outward with their palms up in a gesture of praise (orans position) to pray the Lord's Prayer.

We Go Forth

- Invite children to stand. Lead the closing prayer. As children process back to their seats, have them sing *Songs of Celebration* CD, track 12, "Te alabaré, Señor," or one of the optional music suggestions.

Optional Music Suggestions:

"We Remember," Marty Haugen, © GIA Publications

"One Bread, One Body," © New Dawn, John Foley. Published by OCP

CELEBRATE

Objective

To explore the meaning of the ritual action of kneeling and the words of the Memorial Acclamation

To explain the meaning of the Eucharistic Prayer

Liturgical Catechesis

The purpose of this section is to help children reflect on their experiences of the signs, rituals, prayers, and gestures of the celebration and to lead them to express their own meaning of the experiences. Allow children to share their experiences without commenting on them.

We Remember

- On the board or on chart paper, write the following questions: What did you see? What did you hear? What did you do?
- Guide children to reflect on the celebration by reviewing what happened in the prayer.
- Invite children to share their responses to the questions.

Reflect

- Invite children to complete the phrases with their own thoughts and feelings.
- Remind them that they do not have to complete all three choices.

Kneeling

- Ask children to talk about their experiences of kneeling.
- Invite a volunteer to read the first three sentences.
- Ask children whether there are other ways we use our bodies in prayer. Possible responses: We fold our hands; we close our eyes; we stand; we process.
- Invite children to read the rest of the text silently to find when we kneel during the Mass.

We Remember

SIGNS OF FAITH

Kneeling

We kneel as a sign that we are God's children. When we kneel, we show we depend on God. Kneeling is one of the many ways we use our bodies to pray. Sometimes we kneel when we want to ask God for something. Other times we kneel when we seek God's forgiveness. At Mass we kneel after the Holy, Holy, Holy through the Great Amen. We also kneel during the Lamb of God before Holy Communion.

CELEBRATE

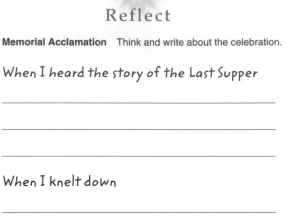

54

Reflect

Memorial Acclamation Think and write about the celebration.

When I heard the story of the Last Supper

_____

_____

_____

When I knelt down

_____

_____

_____

When I prayed "Christ has died, Christ is risen, Christ will come again"

_____

_____

_____

Additional Activity

Create a storyboard Prepare a large poster board or piece of paper. It should be large enough for children to gather around to draw on it. Divide the paper into five parts with the following titles:

We praise you for creation.
We praise you for the people of the Old Testament.
We praise you for Jesus.
We praise you for the Church.
We praise you for us.

Display the storyboard where children can see it.

- Tell children that during Mass we hear the story of all the wonderful gifts God has given humans, and we praise God for those gifts.
- Read each of the titles, and elicit from children what pictures or words might go in each space to describe God's gifts.
- Distribute art materials.
- Invite children to write or draw pictures in the space under the appropriate title.

The Eucharistic Prayer

The Eucharistic Prayer is the Church's great prayer of praise and thanksgiving to God. The priest begins this prayer. Together we pray, "Holy, Holy, Holy." Then we kneel as the prayer continues.

The priest prays to the Holy Spirit to make our gifts holy so they become the Body and Blood of Jesus. He retells the story of the Last Supper. We want to remember what Jesus did for us.

We proclaim the **mystery** of our faith. A mystery of faith is something we believe but we do not understand. We know that Jesus is with us now. We know that all people who love God will live with him in heaven when they die. We believe because Jesus promised us. We want to say, "Thank you."

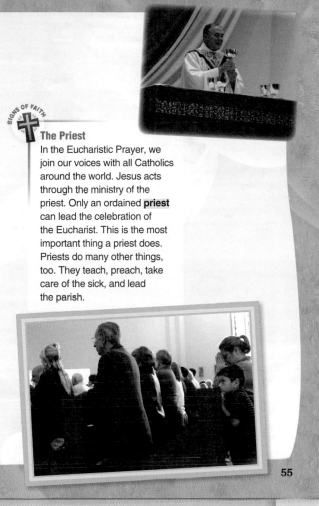

SIGNS OF FAITH

The Priest

In the Eucharistic Prayer, we join our voices with all Catholics around the world. Jesus acts through the ministry of the priest. Only an ordained **priest** can lead the celebration of the Eucharist. This is the most important thing a priest does. Priests do many other things, too. They teach, preach, take care of the sick, and lead the parish.

55

 Teaching Tip

A mystery is a mystery   This chapter touches on the mystery of the Real Presence of Jesus in the Eucharist. Children of this age are concrete thinkers, but they are also able to put ideas together without a lot of explanation. It is not necessary to dwell on the concrete question of how bread and wine are transformed. In fact, if that is the emphasis, children are likely to be skeptical.

It is more important at this age for children to hear that Jesus is present just as he was at the Last Supper when he told his Apostles, "This is my body" and "This is my blood." They will be able to make the connection. Children live and move with mystery more easily than adolescents or adults do.

The Eucharistic Prayer

- Read aloud the first two paragraphs.

- Discuss the word *holy* with children.

- Ask whether anyone remembers how to sing the Holy, Holy, Holy from hearing it during the Mass. If so, sing it together.

- Summarize the last two paragraphs.

- Use the Teaching Tip at the bottom of the page to guide your discussion.

- Emphasize that the Eucharistic Prayer tells the story of God's love for humans and that it is a prayer of thanksgiving.

- Encourage children to listen carefully to the story of the Last Supper as the priest tells it during the Mass next Sunday.

The Priest

- Invite children to read the text silently to find out what is the most important thing a priest does. leads the celebration of the Eucharist

- Be sure children know the name of the parish pastor or other priest. If possible, invite one of the priests to visit your session.

Objective

To explain the significance of the Last Supper

Faith Focus

What does Jesus tell his friends?
List children's responses on the board or on chart paper.

Jesus Gives Thanks

Call attention to the artwork. Have children tell you what is happening. *Jesus is sharing a meal with his Apostles.*

- Recall from the last session the Washing of the Feet Gospel story. Point out that this Gospel story takes place at the Last Supper.

Read aloud the paragraph about the Jewish feast of Passover. Remind children that Jesus would have heard this story when he was about their age.

 Scripture MATTHEW 26:26–28, LUKE 22:14–20

The Last Supper

- Gather children into a story circle or in the prayer space. Remind them that they will be hearing the Gospel story of the Last Supper again.

- Ask what they remember from hearing the Gospel during the celebration.

- Reread the story aloud.

- Or, select some children to dramatize the story. Use the text on pages CE14–15 of this edition.

REMEMBER

Jesus Gives Thanks

Faith Focus

What does Jesus tell his friends?

Long ago, God led the people of Israel out of the land of Egypt where they had been slaves. He saved the people and set them free. Every year at the Passover meal, Jewish people remember and give thanks for God's saving love. They remember God's promises.

MATTHEW 26:26–28 AND LUKE 22:14–20

The Last Supper

On the night before he died, Jesus shared a special meal with his Apostles. They gathered to celebrate the Passover, a great Jewish holiday of thanksgiving.

We call this meal the Last Supper. During the meal, Jesus told his followers how to remember the mystery of our faith.

When it was time to begin, Jesus told his disciples that he had looked forward to eating the Passover meal with them. He knew he would soon suffer.

56

Scripture Background

The Last Supper   Passover is a great Jewish feast. It commemorates the liberation of the Jewish people from slavery in Egypt. The Jewish people continue to celebrate it today as a remembrance of God's liberating presence in history.

It was during the course of a Passover meal that Jesus took the elements of bread and wine. He said, "This is my body" over the bread. Then he took the cup, saying over it, "This is my blood" *(Matthew 26:26–28, Luke 22:14–20)*.

Through this action Jesus initiated something new, namely, a new covenant "for the forgiveness of sins." By partaking of the

Body and Blood of Jesus, Catholics share the blessings of this covenant, receiving forgiveness and liberation from sin. They are empowered to continue to spread the Gospel of salvation and reconciliation.

Jesus then used the bread and wine of the Passover in a new way. While they were eating, Jesus took bread. He said the blessing. He broke the bread. Then he gave the bread to the Apostles. He said, "Take and eat; this is my body."

Then Jesus took a cup of wine. Again he thanked God, his Father. He gave the cup to his disciples and said, "Drink from it. This is my blood, which will be shed for the forgiveness of sins. Whenever you do this, remember me."

BASED ON MATTHEW 26:26–28 AND LUKE 22:14–20

❷ **What did Jesus and his disciples remember at the Passover?**

❷ **How do you remember Jesus?**

Faith at Home

Read the scripture story with your child. Discuss your child's responses to the questions. Talk about ways your family remembers important events, such as patriotic holidays, birthdays, and anniversaries.

Share

Write the message Look at the last paragraph in the story. In the space below, fill in the missing letters to spell Jesus' message

Th__ __   __ __   m__   B__d__.

Th__ __   __ __   m__   Bl__ __d.

Reme__b   __   __ __.

57

✦ Cultural Background

Meals   For the Jewish people, to eat with another was to make a commitment of common ground and friendship with those present at the table. It meant to share "life" with one another. Because a meal was an intimate vehicle of exchange, people tended only to eat with those they trusted or with whom they enjoyed a close relationship. For the most part, people ate only with others of the same social status. These observations make it all the more poignant that Jesus identifies his betrayer as "one who is with me at the table" (Luke 22:21).

- Tell children to listen closely to Jesus' words.
- Ask children what they think Jesus meant when he said, "Remember me."

❷ Discuss the question. Jesus and his followers remembered that God saved his people and set them free in Egypt.

❷ Discuss the question. Possible responses: by helping others; by loving others; by serving God; by going to Mass

✦ Share

Tell children to add letters to complete the message.

- Remind children to look back at the scripture story for hints.
- Have children share their answers.

Review

- Jesus and his Apostles celebrated Passover at the Last Supper.
- Jesus gave us himself at the Last Supper.

Objective

To describe the consecration, Memorial Acclamation, and Great Amen

Faith Focus

What do we remember and give thanks for during the Eucharistic Prayer?
List children's responses on the board or on chart paper.

We Remember and Give Thanks

- Invite a volunteer to read aloud the first paragraph.

- Recall that Catholics come together as a community to worship, and to praise and thank God.

- Summarize the second paragraph, and emphasize the role of the priest as the leader of prayer.

- After summarizing the text, discuss why we pray for one another and for people who have died. Possible responses: We pray for one another because we need help from prayer to live good lives; we pray for those who have died to help them be closer to God.

Blessed Sacrament

- Refer to pages 82–87 in the Words of Faith glossary.

- If possible, visit your parish church to show children where the Blessed Sacrament is reserved in the tabernacle.

We Remember and Give Thanks

SIGNS OF FAITH

Blessed Sacrament
The consecrated Bread and Wine are the Body and Blood of Jesus. They are called the Blessed Sacrament. After Mass the remaining Hosts are placed in a special place called a **tabernacle**. The tabernacle is usually in a chapel or at a side altar in the church. We keep the Blessed Sacrament there so it can be brought to parish members who are ill and cannot be present. We can also spend time before the tabernacle praying to Jesus in the Blessed Sacrament.

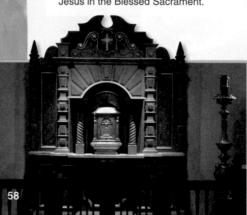

58

Faith Focus

What do we remember and give thanks for during the Eucharistic Prayer?

At the Last Supper, Jesus and the disciples remembered the Passover story. They said special prayers of thanks. We call the Eucharist "The Lord's Supper."

During the Eucharistic Prayer, the priest joins all of our prayers into one. He prays in our name and the name of the Church. We take part in the prayer, too. During the prayer, we remember all the ways that God has saved us. We offer ourselves to God with Jesus. We share in Jesus' dying and rising through the power of the Holy Spirit. We remember and we say, "Thank you."

The priest asks God to accept our sacrifice. We pray that God will make us holy, like the saints who are in heaven with him. We pray for one another. We offer the Mass for the people who have died.

✦ Catechist Background

Eucharistic Prayers used for Masses with children The Sacramentary (Roman Missal) contains three Eucharistic Prayers approved for use in Masses celebrated with children. These prayers are written in a language that encourages the development of a child's religious experience while keeping the dignity of the prayer. They also provide for an active participation of children during the Eucharistic Prayer.

- The first Eucharistic Prayer is the simplest. It emphasizes thanksgiving and has a sense of wonder and joy. It is the one most helpful for children just beginning to celebrate the Eucharist.

- The second Eucharistic Prayer is more of a dialogue. It contains several Acclamations.

- The third Eucharistic Prayer has an Easter focus. Its tone is one of joy and thanksgiving.

If your religious education program does a special celebration of the Eucharist with groups of children or with children and their families, encourage the use of one of these prayers.

Consecration

An important part of the Eucharistic Prayer is the **consecration**. The priest says the words Jesus did at the Last Supper. Through the power of the Holy Spirit and the words and actions of the priest, the gifts of bread and wine become the Body and Blood of Christ.

After the consecration we remember that Jesus gave his life for us. The priest says or sings: "Let us proclaim the mystery of faith." We answer with a special response. This response is the Memorial Acclamation.

The Great Amen

At the end of the Eucharistic Prayer, the priest prays the prayer that begins,

"Through him, with him, and in him."

We answer, "Amen."

This response is the Great Amen. We say "yes" to God's promises. We praise him for his gifts and saving actions.

? How is the Eucharist like the Last Supper?

Faith at Home

Review your child's response to the question. Go over the meaning of the word *Amen*. Go through the Eucharistic Prayer on these pages with your child. Familiarize your child with the responses to the prayer.

59

⬧ Sacrament Background

Doxology The Eucharistic Prayer ends with a prayer often called the Great Amen. However, "Amen" is an immediate response to a doxology, which is a prayer expressing glory to the triune God, the Trinity—Father, Son, and Holy Spirit.

It has been customary from earliest times that all public prayer closes with praise of God. Historically consistent, the doxology reminds us of the essential purpose of all prayer: we bow before our Creator.

No matter what form the Eucharistic Prayer has taken through the ages, the doxology has always been its conclusion and the wording of the doxology has always been emphatic. Here around this altar and table, God does receive honor and praise.

Consecration

Write the terms *consecration, Memorial Acclamation,* and *Great Amen* on the board or on chart paper. As you define each term, invite a child to come up and place a check mark next to the term.

- Read the text aloud, and help children recall when the consecration occurs during the Mass.
- Use the photograph to show the priest's gestures during the consecration.
- If your parish customarily uses a particular Memorial Acclamation, help the children recall it, and practice it as a group.

The Great Amen

- Remind children that *Amen* means "so be it" or "yes."
- Read the text aloud to show the significance of this prayer.

? Discuss the question. Possible responses: It is a gathering of people who love Jesus; it is a meal; it is a remembrance of Jesus' love for us; it is a prayer.

Activity Master

You may wish to use Activity Master 6 on page CE14 to guide children in naming what they want to thank God for and for whom they want to pray.

▲ Activity Master 6

Review

- We recall the Last Supper at the Eucharist.
- The consecration, the Memorial Acclamation, and the Great Amen are part of the Eucharistic Prayer.

Objective

To help children remember and give thanks for gifts from God

Say "Yes"

Respond

Explain the activity to children.

- Help children locate the *a* and *b* spaces.
- Recall what stained-glass windows look like in your church, or show them a picture of stained glass.
- Distribute art materials.
- Begin the activity, and give children a time limit.
- Move through the room, and help when needed.

Closing Blessing

- Gather children into a prayer circle with their books.
- Begin with the Sign of the Cross.
- Read aloud the People of Faith story about Paschal Baylon.
- Pray the prayer.
- End with the *Songs of Celebration* CD, track 12, "Te alabaré, Señor," or one of the optional music suggestions on page 53.

Say "Yes"

Respond

Make a stained glass window In the picture below, color the spaces with an "a" yellow. Color the spaces with a "b" red. Choose another color to fill in the areas marked with "c" to complete the stained-glass window. Then write one way you can say "yes" to Jesus this week.

Closing Blessing

Gather and begin with the Sign of the Cross.

Leader: God, our Father, we remember and give thanks for all your good gifts.

All: Amen.

Leader: Jesus, our Savior, we remember and give thanks for your death and Resurrection.

All: Amen.

Leader: Holy Spirit, we remember and give thanks that you are with us.

All: Amen.

Sing together.

Te alabaré, Señor; tú me has librado.

I will praise you Lord; you have rescued me.

Tony Alonso © 2003 GIA Pub, Inc.

60

✦ People of Faith: A Read Aloud Story

Paschal Baylon Paschal was born in France on Pentecost Sunday. His family named him Paschal because he was born during the Easter season. Another name for the Easter season is the Paschal season. As a boy Paschal helped his father on the family farm. He took care of the sheep. Paschal taught himself to read. He loved to pray to Jesus in the Blessed Sacrament. He became a Franciscan lay brother, often serving as a cook or doorkeeper. As an adult he kept his great love of the Eucharist and helped other people believe that Jesus is present in the Eucharist.

C. 1540–1592

Faith Focus

- The Eucharistic Prayer is a prayer of thanksgiving, remembering, and consecration.

- Through the power of the Holy Spirit and the words and actions of the priest, the bread and wine become the Body and Blood of Jesus.

- At the Great Amen, the assembly says "yes" to all of God's saving actions and promises.

Ritual Focus

Memorial Acclamation The celebration focused on the Memorial Acclamation. The children prayed the Acclamation. During the week, use the Family Prayer as a prayer before or after meals.

www.harcourtreligion.com
Visit our Web site for weekly scripture readings and questions, family resources, and more activities.

Act

Share Together Talk about ways your family remembers people who have moved away or died. Use examples of pictures or stories to get the sharing started. Make a list of the examples that family members share. Use the list to talk about ways your family can remember Jesus during the week.

Do Together Plan a time to make a visit to the Blessed Sacrament with your child. Your parish church may have a Blessed Sacrament chapel set apart from the body of the church. Go near the place where the tabernacle is located. Spend some quiet time in conversation with Jesus in the Blessed Sacrament.

Family Prayer

Giving God, we give you thanks for all the gifts you give us: for the gifts of creation, for family and friends, and especially for the gift of your Son, Jesus. Help us to always remember that you are here with us. Amen.

Faith at Home

Review the five parts of the Faith at Home page with children.

Encourage children:

- to ask family members to review the **Faith Focus** statements

- to share the **Ritual Focus: Memorial Acclamation** with family members

- to do at least one of the **Act** activities with family members

- to pray the **Family Prayer** with their family at times when the family is together

- to encourage their family members to go to **www.harcourtreligion.com** with them and do the activities for this chapter sometime during the week

Looking Ahead

For Chapter 7, you will need:

- a Bible

- a prayer table

- a candle

- the *Songs of Celebration* CD

- copies of Activity Master 7 on p. CE17 for each child

- copies of the Scripture Narration 7 on pp. CE18–19 for participants

- healthy refreshments, such as juice, bread, and fruit, for the celebration

7 We Share a Meal

General Instruction of the Roman Missal

"Since the Eucharistic Celebration is the Paschal Banquet, it is desirable that in keeping with the Lord's command, his Body and Blood should be received as spiritual food by the faithful who are properly disposed." (no. 80)

Catechism Connection

To deepen your own background and reflection on the Eucharist as a meal, refer to the *Catechism of the Catholic Church, 1382–1398*.

Catechist Resources

 Children Discover the Mass: Lessons, Crafts, Cutouts, and More
Mary Doerfler Dall
Ave Maria Press
Contains many hands-on projects relating to the Mass

 The Welcome Table: Planning Masses with Children
Elizabeth McMahon Jeep et al.
Liturgy Training Publications
Help for teaching children about liturgy as you plan Mass together

Children's Resources

 We Feed (12 min)
St. Anthony Messenger Press.
A delightful story of that shows how Eucharist feeds hunger.

 The Tortilla Factory*
Gary Paulsen
Voyager Books
Traces the cycle of life from seed to plant to tortilla

 * *Available at* **www.harcourtreligion.com**

Catechist Formation

"And I have given them the glory you gave me, so that they may be one, as we are one."

John 17:22

Meals and Communion

The times when families gather together for a meal are treasured moments. Sharing a meal provides a time for families to bond. Time together around the table provides nourishment for both body and spirit.

The Sunday gathering for Eucharist enables members of the Church family to realize their oneness with Christ and with one another. The celebration of the Eucharist as both meal and sacrifice centers on the union of the assembly with Christ through Communion. Before approaching the Table of the Lord to receive Holy Communion, those gathered pray the Lord's Prayer and share the Sign of Peace with one another to acknowledge the importance of being one.

Meals and Faith

With the reception of Holy Communion, the Amen of the communicants acknowledges that they believe Christ is present under the appearances of bread and wine. They believe that through sharing in Holy Communion, Christ is transforming them and the whole Church into the Body of Christ. Communion is a sign of the intimate link that Christ has with every believer. It is also a sign that the Church stands together to witness to the world as a community of Christ's love for all.

What signs remind you that you are growing in a deeper union with Christ?

What unique gifts do you bring to the Body of Christ, the Church?

Catechist Prayer

Heavenly Father, thank you for the gift of your Son in the Eucharist. Deepen my oneness with him. Help me follow his example. Amen.

Lesson Planner

www.harcourtreligion.com
Visit our Web site for additional
resources and information.

		OBJECTIVES	LESSON PROCESS	ACTIVITIES	MATERIALS
CELEBRATE	10 minutes Pages 62–63	Ritual Focus *Sharing a Meal* To experience a celebration of the word, including Sharing a Meal	Celebrate the opening prayer.		PROGRAM RESOURCES *Songs of Celebration* CD, track 13 OTHER MATERIALS Bible, cross, prayer table, candle, large glass bowl filled with water, simple healthy refreshments, table and chairs for the meal, eating utensils
	Pages 64–65	To explore the meaning of the ritual action To explain that the Eucharist is the Church's special meal	Reflect on the celebration. Complete the activity. Reflect on why we share meals. ✝ Read about and discuss The Sign of Peace. Describe the Eucharist as the Church's meal. ✝ Read about and discuss the paten, chalice, and ciborium.	☀ **Reflect** Children reflect on the experience of the celebration and the meaning of Sharing a Meal.	
REMEMBER	30 minutes Pages 66–67	Faith Focus *What does Jesus tell us about himself?* To explain the connection between the Eucharist and eternal life	Recall the significance of Biblical meals. 📖 Proclaim the Gospel story. *John 6:30–58* Complete the activity.	☀ **Share** Children draw one way Jesus gives us what we need. ▰ **Faith at Home** Suggested activities for the home	PROGRAM RESOURCES Copies of Activity Master 7, p. CE17 Copies of Scripture Narration 7, pp. CE18–19
	Pages 68–69	Faith Focus *What happens during the Communion Rite?* To describe what happens during the Communion Rite	Identify the components of the Communion Rite. Explain the correct procedure for receiving Holy Communion. ✝ Read about and discuss the Lamb of God prayer.	▰ **Faith at Home** Suggested activities for the home	
LIVE	20 minutes Page 70	To reflect on the meaning of Holy Communion	Introduce the activity. Pray the Closing Blessing. Read aloud the People of Faith story about Venerable Maria Teresa Quevedo.	☀ **Respond** Children write a prayer.	PROGRAM RESOURCES *Songs of Celebration* CD, track 13
FAITH AT HOME	Page 71	▰ **Faith at Home** To introduce the different parts of the Faith at Home page	Review the Faith at Home page. Encourage children to share this page at home.	☀ **Act** Suggested activities for the home	PROGRAM RESOURCES Family Guide, pp. 28–29

CELEBRATE

Objective

To experience a celebration of the word, including Sharing a Meal.

Preparation

Familiarize yourself with the movements of the ritual focus for Sharing a Meal on page 63. You will need:

- a Bible
- a cross
- a table covered with a white cloth
- a candle and a large glass bowl filled with water on the prayer table
- simple healthy refreshments, such as bread, grape juice, fruit
- a table and chairs for the meal
- eating utensils

 Use the *Songs of Celebration* CD, track 13, to rehearse the suggested song, "Come to the Table," or one of the optional music suggestions on page 63.

Select a child to carry the Bible in procession.

We Gather

Invite children to assemble with their books.

Gather children into the prayer space with a procession.

- Have children follow you and the child carrying the Bible, as you lead the procession.

 As you process, lead children in singing using the *Songs of Celebration* CD, track 13.

- When all are assembled, light the prayer candle.
- Begin prayer, and lead children in the Sign of the Cross.

Follow the order of prayer on pages 62–63.

We Gather

Procession

As you sing, walk forward slowly. Follow the person carrying the Bible. Gather around the table.

 Sing together.

> We come to the Table of the Lord
> As one body formed in your love.
> We come to the Table of the Lord
> As one body formed in your love.
>
> © 2004 John Burland

Leader: Let us pray.

Make the Sign of the Cross together.

62

We Listen

Leader: God, our Father, you provide us with everything we need. Strengthen us to bring life to others. We ask this through Jesus Christ our Lord.

All: Amen.

Leader: A reading from the holy Gospel according to John.

All: Glory to you, Lord.

Trace the Sign of the Cross on your forehead, lips, and heart.

Leader: Read John 6:30–58.

The Gospel of the Lord.

All: Praise to you, Lord Jesus Christ.

Sit silently.

✷ Ritual Background

Sharing food Eating and drinking are ritual-laden human activities. The way we eat and drink reflects the customs of our culture and society. Sharing food can also have religious significance, as it does, for example, in the Jewish Passover meal or in the breaking of the Muslim fast during the month of Ramadan.

The Eucharist is a sacrifice and the sacred meal of our salvation. As a meal, the Eucharist taps into a deep reservoir of human experience concerning the sharing of food. We participate with care and respect for our brothers and sisters.

When Saint Paul chastised the community at Corinth, he pointed to their selfish behavior at table as a sign that they did not fully understand the Eucharist (*1 Corinthians 11:17–22*).

Ritual Focus: Sharing a Meal

Be seated around the table.

Leader: Blessed are you, almighty Father,

who gives us our daily bread.

Blessed is your only begotten Son,

who continually feeds us with the word of life.

Blessed is the Holy Spirit,

who brings us together at this table of love.

Blessed be God now and for ever.

All: Amen.

BOOK OF BLESSINGS, 1069

Share the food at the table.

Leader: We give you thanks for all your gifts, almighty God, living and reigning now and for ever.

All: Amen.

BOOK OF BLESSINGS, 1070

We Go Forth

Leader: Loving God, we thank you for food, for families, for friends, and for the gift of your Son, Jesus. Help us to share the gifts of life with others. We ask this in the name of your Son, Jesus.

All: Amen.

 Sing the opening song together.

63

Liturgical Background

Sign of Peace   In the ancient Church the Sign of Peace was a kiss. More than simply a gesture of Christian affection, the kiss indicated a mutual sharing of the Spirit of Christ. This gesture was common to the early Christian community. It was used at the conclusion of prayer and at the conclusion of initiation and ordination rites to affirm everything that went before it.

Today, the kiss of peace is modified out of respect for modern sensibilities about touch. Usually the gesture is a hand clasp, a hug, or something similar, rather than a kiss.

We share the Sign of Peace in a way that includes those around us equally, because it is an acknowledgment of the peace Christ gives to all. The Sign of Peace does not "come from the altar" as it did in the late Middle Ages, but it is exchanged immediately within the congregation, once the invitation is given. It is a sign of solidarity and commitment with one another before coming to the table.

We Listen

For the proclamation of the Gospel, you may use a Bible or the adapted reading in the *Child's Book* on pages 66–67.

Ritual Focus: Sharing a Meal

- Direct the children to gather around the table and be seated.
- Pray the Blessing Prayer.
- Share the meal.
- At the end of the meal, gather children around the prayer table.
- Invite children to exchange the Sign of Peace.

We Go Forth

- Lead the closing prayer. As children return to their seats, have them sing *Songs of Celebration* CD, track 13, "Come to the Table," or one of the optional music suggestions.

Optional Music Suggestions:

"Canción del Cuerpo de Cristo," David Haas/trad. Hawaiian melody/trans. Donna Pena © GIA Publications

"Let Us Break Bread Together," African-American Traditional

CELEBRATE

Objective

To explore the meaning of the ritual action of Sharing a Meal

To explain that the Eucharist is the Church's special meal

Liturgical Catechesis

The purpose of this section is to help children reflect on their experiences of the signs, rituals, prayers, and gestures of the celebration and to lead them to express their own meaning of the experiences. Allow children to share their experiences without commenting on them.

Special Meals

- On the board or on chart paper, write the following questions: What did you see? What did you hear? What did you do?

- Guide children to reflect on the celebration by reviewing what happened in the prayer and as they shared food.

- Invite children to share their responses to the questions.

Reflect

- Invite children to complete the phrases with their own thoughts and feelings.

- Invite volunteers to share their responses.

Sign of Peace

- Ask children to read the text silently. Tell them to read to find out what giving the Sign of Peace means. We are united with one another at the Table of the Lord.

- Practice the Sign of Peace with children.

Special Meals

CELEBRATE

SIGNS OF FAITH

Sign of Peace
During Mass we offer one another the **Sign of Peace** before Holy Communion. The Sign of Peace is an action prayer. We reach out our hand to people around us. We wish them God's peace. Giving the Sign of Peace to others is a sign that we are united to one another at the Table of the Lord.

64

Reflect

Sharing a meal Think and write about the celebration.

I like sharing meals with others because

_____

_____

_____

When I eat good food

_____

_____

Bread reminds me of

_____

_____

_____

⬟ Additional Activity

Make a list Gather children for a brainstorming activity. Write the statement, "The best things about sharing a meal are…" on the board or on chart paper.

- Ask children to volunteer as many responses as they can.

- Write their responses on the board or on chart paper.

- When they have finished, make connections between their responses and the image of the Eucharist as a meal.

The best things

The Eucharist as a Meal

Sharing a meal brings people closer together. A special meal, sometimes called a banquet or feast, is a time to celebrate. It is a time to share stories, sing songs, and eat special food. When families and friends gather for special meals, they grow in love.

The Eucharist is the Church's special meal. The Holy Spirit gathers us with our parish family and with Catholics all over the world. We gather at the Eucharist to celebrate God's love for us. We also share Jesus' own Body and Blood in Holy Communion. Jesus is truly present in both the consecrated Bread and the Wine.

Jesus is the Bread of Life. In the meal of the Eucharist, we share in the life of the Risen Christ.

SIGNS OF FAITH

Paten, Ciborium, and Chalice
The food for our Eucharistic meal is placed on special dishes. The **paten** holds the large host. The smaller hosts are carried in a **ciborium**. The wine is poured into a **chalice**.

65

Teaching Tip

Guidelines for receiving Communion Remind children about these guidelines for receiving Communion:

1. If we have committed a serious sin, we must celebrate the Sacrament of Reconciliation before receiving Communion.

2. We do not eat or drink anything except water for one hour before receiving Communion.

3. How we act and the way we dress for Mass should show respect for Jesus' presence in the Eucharist.

4. We are encouraged to receive Holy Communion at every Eucharist we attend, unless we have committed a serious sin.

The Eucharist as a Meal

- Read the first paragraph aloud.
- Ask children what special meals their families share.
- Invite volunteers to tell why the meal they chose is special.
- Read aloud the second paragraph.
- Point out that Catholics all over the world share in the meal of the Eucharist.
- Invite children to silently reread the paragraph to find two reasons the Eucharist is a special meal.
- Invite volunteers to share their reasons. Possible responses: The Holy Spirit gathers us; we celebrate God's love; we share Jesus' own body and blood.
- Read the final paragraph aloud.

Paten, Ciborium, and Chalice

- Refer to pages 82–87 in the Words of Faith glossary.
- Invite children to read the text silently to find out what the difference is between the chalice and the ciborium. The chalice holds the Blood of Christ, and the ciborium holds his Body.
- Show children that the paten holds the large host the priest uses during Mass and the ciborium holds the smaller hosts we receive during Holy Communion.

Objective

To explain the connection between the Eucharist and eternal life

Faith Focus

What does Jesus tell us about himself?

List children's responses on the board or on chart paper.

We Share the Bread of Life

Recall with children different meals Jesus shared with others. Summarize the miracle of the loaves and fish.

- Call attention to the illustration. Point out that it pictures only a few of the people Jesus fed and taught.

- Point out that Jesus will feed us, just as he fed the crowd.

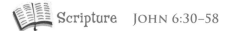 Scripture   JOHN 6:30–58

I Am the Bread of Life

- Gather children into a story circle or in the prayer space. Remind them that they will be hearing the story from the Gospel of John again.

- Ask what they remember from hearing the Gospel during the celebration.

- Reread the story aloud.

- Or, select some children to narrate the story. Use the text on pages CE18–19 of this edition.

Have children listen so that they can tell you what Jesus is telling the people about himself. He is the Bread of Life.

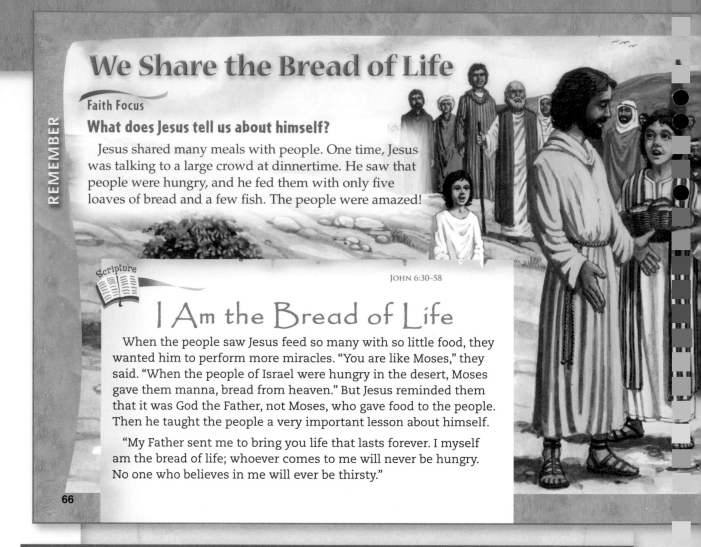

We Share the Bread of Life

Faith Focus

What does Jesus tell us about himself?

Jesus shared many meals with people. One time, Jesus was talking to a large crowd at dinnertime. He saw that people were hungry, and he fed them with only five loaves of bread and a few fish. The people were amazed!

Scripture

JOHN 6:30–58

I Am the Bread of Life

When the people saw Jesus feed so many with so little food, they wanted him to perform more miracles. "You are like Moses," they said. "When the people of Israel were hungry in the desert, Moses gave them manna, bread from heaven." But Jesus reminded them that it was God the Father, not Moses, who gave food to the people. Then he taught the people a very important lesson about himself.

"My Father sent me to bring you life that lasts forever. I myself am the bread of life; whoever comes to me will never be hungry. No one who believes in me will ever be thirsty."

66

Scripture Background

Signs of Divinity   The Gospel according to John more clearly expresses Jesus' claims to divinity than the other Gospels do.

Jesus' listeners understood the "I am" phrase in the light of the revelation of God's own name to Moses in the burning bush *(Exodus 3:14)*. When Moses wondered by what authority he was sent to the Egyptian pharaoh, God answered that Moses should tell the pharaoh that "I am" sent him. Because of this understanding, some of those who heard him accused Jesus of blasphemy.

An example of this claim is then used throughout the Gospel according to John where Jesus also performs signs so that people will recognize his identity. The sign of the multiplication of the loaves and fish points to the reality that Jesus himself is manna to feed the people. What the people did not understand at that time was that Jesus and the Father were one.

Jesus continued, "I am the bread from heaven. The people who ate manna in the desert eventually died, as all humans die. But if you share my own flesh and blood, I will always be with you. You will live forever with God."

"What is he talking about?" some people asked. Jesus answered them, "Whoever shares in my life will live forever. Just as the Father sent me and I have life because of him, so too will the one who eats the Bread of Life have life."

BASED ON JOHN 6:30–58

Faith at Home

Read the scripture story with your child. Make connections between the effects of food for our physical bodies and Jesus as the food for our spirit. Together, decide on one activity you can do this week to remember that Jesus is the Bread of Life.

❓ **What do you think Jesus means when he says he is the Bread of Life?**

❓ **How can you share in Jesus' life?**

Share

Draw a picture Draw one way Jesus gives you what you need to live.

67

❓ Discuss the question. He is our food; he will nourish us.

❓ Discuss the question. by going to Holy Communion

Share

- Have children work alone on the activity.

- Explain the activity to children, and set a time limit.

- Walk among the group, and offer suggestions as needed.

- Have children share their work.

Cultural Background

Bread In Jesus' time, bread was usually made from either wheat or barley. Bread made from barley was the bread for those who were poor. However, bread might also be made by mixing grains such as lentils, beans, and millet. The best bread was made from wheat in which only the grain was ground and the bran was not used. Bread was baked either on hot stones, on an iron griddle, or in an oven heated with twigs or grass.

Bread is always included in the major Jewish religious feasts. In the Gospel of John, this Bread of Life discourse takes place around the time of the feast of Passover.

Review

- Jesus is the Bread of Life.

- God gives us life that will last forever.

Objective

To describe what happens at the Communion Rite

Faith Focus

What happens during the Communion Rite?
List children's responses on the board or on chart paper.

The Communion Rite

Remind children that they will soon be receiving Jesus for the first time in Holy Communion. Read each bulleted statement to children. Stop after each statement, and have children paraphrase it.

- Read the paragraph about preparing to receive Holy Communion. Point out that by learning about this sacrament, children are preparing for Holy Communion.

- Ask children how we prepare at Mass to receive Communion. We pray the Lord's Prayer; we remember we are all part of God's family; we share the Sign of Peace.

Lamb of God

- Read the text aloud.

- Read aloud the Lamb of God prayer on page 116 in this edition. Have them repeat the prayer after you. You can also have the children turn to page 90 of their books for the prayer.

The Communion Rite

SIGNS OF FAITH

Lamb of God
The **Lamb of God** is a title for Jesus. This title reminds us that Jesus gave up his life for our sins. When we pray or sing this prayer before Holy Communion, we remember that through Jesus' death and Resurrection our sins are forgiven and we have peace.

Faith Focus

What happens during the Communion Rite?

We receive Jesus, the Bread of Life, in Holy Communion. What does this mean?

- We are united to Jesus.

- Our friendship with Jesus grows stronger.

- God forgives our less serious sins if we are sorry and gives us strength to avoid serious sin.

- We are united with the whole Church, the Body of Christ.

- We share in God's promise that we will live in heaven with Jesus, Mary, and all the saints.

We prepare ourselves to receive Holy Communion. Together we stand and pray the Lord's Prayer. We remember we are one family with God. As a sign of unity, we share the Sign of Peace with each other.

68

 ## Catechist Background

Real Presence After the consecration, Jesus is truly and fully present under the appearances of both bread and wine. His presence—Body and Blood, soul and divinity—remains in the consecrated Bread and Wine after the celebration of the Eucharist is over. This is one reason why we reserve the Blessed Sacrament in the tabernacle after Mass. The doctrine of Real Presence is a doctrine of faith. As Saint Thomas Aquinas said, it "cannot be apprehended by the senses but only by faith" (*Summa Theologica IIIa, 9. 75, a. 1.*).

- Although children are concrete thinkers, they also possess a sense of faith and mystery that usually enables them to grasp the meaning of the doctrine when simple phrases such as "This is Jesus" or "This is the Body and Blood of Jesus" are used without attempting to explain the "how."

- One of the primary criteria to discern children's readiness to receive Holy Communion for the first time is that they know the difference between the consecrated Bread we share at Eucharist and ordinary bread.

Holy Communion

During Holy Communion, the priest invites us to the table. He reminds us of Jesus' sacrifice and presence in the Eucharist. He holds up the large Host and says, "This is the Lamb of God, who takes away the sins of the world. Happy are those who are called to his supper." We come forward in a procession. Sometimes we sing.

When it is our turn to receive Jesus, we cup our hands with one hand on top of the other. The priest, deacon, or extraordinary minister of Holy Communion says, "The body of Christ." We answer, "Amen."

Often, we may also receive from the cup. After we swallow the Host, we go to the deacon or extraordinary minister of Holy Communion, who offers the cup and says, "The blood of Christ." We answer, "Amen." We return to our places. We pray or sing a prayer of thanksgiving.

We should receive Holy Communion every time we participate in the Mass. We must do so at least once a year.

❓ **Why are we happy to share in the Lord's Supper?**

Faith at Home

Review your child's response to the question. Talk about what happens when we receive Holy Communion by referring to the list on page 68. Use this page to show your child how to go to Holy Communion.

69

✸ Sacrament Background

Communion under both species   In the very early Church, receiving Communion under both species was normal. The fact that the Eucharist had its beginnings in the Passover meal, and in other fraternal meals that included rituals around bread and wine, shaped this custom.

When the practice of fully initiating infants became the norm, the practice developed in many churches of giving infants a small piece of the consecrated Bread and a sip of consecrated Wine. When an infant could not swallow the consecrated Bread, the child was given Communion with a sip of consecrated Wine.

The practice of Communion under both species was discouraged during times of plague because of the fear of contagion from using the communal cup. However, the practice was restored in the liturgical renewal after the Second Vatican Council and continues today under the direction of local bishops *(GIRM 283)*.

Holy Communion

Write the terms *Host* and *extraordinary minister* on the board or on chart paper. Define these terms as you discuss the information on the page.

- Invite children to study the photograph as you read the text.

- Demonstrate the correct way to receive Holy Communion, and give children time to practice receiving the Host and cup.

- Ask why we pray a prayer of thanksgiving after receiving Communion. Because we are happy to have received Jesus, we thank Jesus for all the gifts he gives us.

❓ Read and discuss the question. Accept all reasonable responses.

Activity Master

You may wish to use Activity Master 7 on page CE17 to review the order of steps in receiving the Eucharist.

▲ Activity Master 7

Review

- We receive Jesus in Holy Communion during the Communion Rite.

- Priests and extraordinary ministers of Holy Communion distribute Communion to us.

Objective

To reflect on the meaning of Holy Communion

Receive Jesus

Respond

Explain the activity to children.

- Explain that this is a private prayer that they can share if they wish.

- Walk among children, offering assistance.

- Ask volunteers to share their prayers.

Closing Blessing

- Gather children into a prayer circle with their books.

- Begin with the Sign of the Cross.

- Read the story of Venerable Maria Teresa Quevedo.

- Pray the prayer.

 End with *Songs of Celebration* CD, track 13, "Come to the Table," or one of the optional music suggestions on page 63.

Receive Jesus

Respond

Write a prayer   In the space below, write a prayer. Share your thoughts and feelings about receiving Jesus for the first time in Holy Communion.

_____

_____

_____

_____

_____

_____

_____

Closing Blessing

Gather and begin with the Sign of the Cross.

Leader: God, our Father, we praise and thank you for the gift of life.

All: Amen.

Leader: Jesus, our Savior, we praise and thank you for giving yourself to us in Holy Communion.

All: Amen.

Leader: Holy Spirit, giver of God's gifts, we praise and thank you for helping us live as members of the Body of Christ.

All: Amen.

Sing together.

We come to the Table of the Lord
As one body formed in your love.
We come to the Table of the Lord
As one body formed in your love.

© 2004 John Burland

✷ People of Faith: A Read Aloud Story

Venerable Maria Teresa Quevedo   Maria Teresa was born in Spain. When she was three, Maria Teresa's mother said: "She is a bundle of happiness. Everyone loves her. She is pretty as a picture but terribly self-willed. She cannot be crossed." Maria Teresa was a picky eater. Sometimes she was rude to others and would not say she was sorry when she hurt them. After her First Communion, her parents noticed that she changed. She began to be kind and loving toward others. As she grew up, Maria Teresa kept her happy spirit and made many friends. When she was eleven years old, she wrote in her notebook, "I have decided to become a saint." She lived a short life, but she used the time to become close to Jesus.

C. 1930–1950

Faith Focus

- The Mass is a meal of thanksgiving.

- Jesus is the Bread of Life.

- In Holy Communion we are united to Jesus and the Church. We share in the promise of life forever with God.

Ritual Focus

Sharing a Meal The celebration focused on Sharing a Meal. The children prayed a blessing prayer and shared food. During the week, use the Blessing Prayer on page 63 as the prayer before your main meal.

www.harcourtreligion.com
Visit our Web site for weekly scripture readings and questions, family resources, and more activities.

Act

Share Together As a family, share a special meal of remembering and celebration. Encourage each member to bring pictures, symbols, or souvenirs of his or her favorite time as a family. Share the memories during the meal, and end the meal with a family prayer.

Do Together As a family, prepare a meal for an elderly couple or a family where a parent is sick or a new baby has arrived. Plan the meal, contact the family to choose a convenient time, prepare the meal, and deliver it. As an option, volunteer to serve meals at a soup kitchen or Catholic Worker house.

Family Prayer

Lord, thank you for all the gifts you have given us. Thank you for family and friends. Help us grow strong in love for one another and for you. Send us the Holy Spirit to show us how to share your life and love with others. Amen.

71

Faith at Home

Review the five parts of the Faith at Home page with children.

Encourage children:

- to ask family members to review the **Faith Focus** statements

- to share the **Ritual Focus: Sharing a Meal** with family members

- to do at least one of the  **Act** activities with family members

- to pray the **Family Prayer** with their family at times when the family is together

- to encourage their family members to go to **www.harcourtreligion.com** with them and do the activities for this chapter sometime during the week

Looking Ahead

For Chapter 8, you will need:

- a Bible

- a prayer table

 the *Songs of Celebration* CD

- copies of Activity Master 8 on p. CE20 for each child

- copies of the Scripture Drama 8 on pp. CE21–22 for participants

General Instruction of the Roman Missal

The Concluding Rite includes "the dismissal of the people by the deacon or the priest so that each may go out to do good works, praising and blessing God." (no. 90)

Catechism Connection

To deepen your own background and reflection on the fruits of Holy Communion, refer to the *Catechism of the Catholic Church, 1391–1397.*

Catechist Resources

 Introducing Catholic Social Teaching to Children with Stories and Activities*
Anne E. Neuberger
Twenty-Third Publications
Uses stories to foster awareness of justice

 This Sacred People: Living the Mystery of Faith*
(21 min)
Daniel Connors
Twenty-Third Publications
Discusses how to live the Eucharist in daily life

Children's Resources

 The Catholic Kid's Guide to Stewardship*
Elizabeth M. Johnson
Twenty-Third Publications
Uses true stories to spark children's desire to live out the corporal works of mercy

 To Live as Jesus Did *(15 min)*
Gaynell Cronin
St. Anthony Messenger Press
Inspires children to live a life of service, as Jesus did

 Available at **www.harcourtreligion.com**

Catechist Formation

> "Go, therefore, and make disciples
> of all nations..."
>
> Matthew 28:19

Going Forth

Usually when people receive an assignment or task to carry out, some words of encouragement help to instill confidence as they move forward with the assigned project. The duty to carry out a task does not have to be seen as a burden; it can be seen as recognition that the person who receives the task has the gifts and ability to carry out a certain responsibility.

This kind of thinking underlies the Concluding Rite of the Mass, when people are blessed and sent into the world as disciples of Christ. Even though Mass comes to a conclusion, its impact and meaning continue as those who have shared in the Eucharist serve as a blessing for others in their lives in the world. Those gathered for the Eucharist do not only receive Christ for their own sake. They take the Body and Blood of Christ into their hearts and are transformed so that they can be witnesses of Christ to others in the world through their words and actions.

Apostolic Witness

In this way, they carry on the mission of the Apostles whom Christ sent out to all the nations to proclaim the good news (*Matthew 28:19*). Catholics are sent out from Mass in the same way, with a blessing that instills courage and confidence, and with a responsibility that assures God's message of salvation will continue to be visible in the world. This responsibility includes deepening their union with Christ, a commitment to the poor, and working for the unity of Christians.

How does your participation in Sunday Mass affect your life?

In what ways do you see the Church reaching out to others in the world?

Catechist Prayer

Almighty God, deepen in me a spirit of discipleship. May the Sacrament of the Eucharist help me to live the values of the Gospel in every word and action. Amen.

Lesson Planner

		OBJECTIVES	LESSON PROCESS	ACTIVITIES	MATERIALS
CELEBRATE	15 minutes Pages 72–73	Ritual Focus *Blessing for Mission* To experience a celebration of the word, including a Blessing for Mission	Celebrate the opening prayer.		PROGRAM RESOURCES *Songs of Celebration* CD, track 14 OTHER MATERIALS Bible, prayer table, candle, large glass bowl filled with water
	Pages 74–75	To explore the meaning of the ritual action To teach that we are sent forth from Mass to carry God's love to others	Reflect on the celebration. Complete the activity. Read about and discuss blessing. Describe our mission as followers of Jesus. Read about and discuss mission and witness.	**Reflect** Children reflect on the experience of the celebration and the meaning of being blessed for mission.	
REMEMBER	30 minutes Pages 76–77	Faith Focus *What happens when we receive the Holy Spirit?* To explain that the Holy Spirit is in our lives today	Discuss why and how the Holy Spirit helps us today. Proclaim the Gospel story of Pentecost. *Acts 2:1–41* Complete the activity.	**Share** Children write a rhyme. **Faith at Home** Suggested activities for the home	PROGRAM RESOURCES Copies of Activity Master 8, p. CE20 Copies of Scripture Drama 8, pp. CE21–22
	Pages 78–79	Faith Focus *How do we love and serve Jesus?* To explain why we are sent forth from Mass	Identify tasks that the Holy Spirit helps us with. Read about and discuss the role of deacons. Discuss how we are sent forth from Mass.	**Faith at Home** Suggested activities for the home	
LIVE	15 minutes Page 80	To reinforce the concept of service	Introduce the activity. Pray the Closing Blessing. Read aloud the People of Faith story about Saint Therese of Lisieux.	**Respond** Children write a story about serving others.	PROGRAM RESOURCES *Songs of Celebration* CD, track 14
FAITH AT HOME	Page 81	**Faith at Home** To introduce the different parts of the Faith at Home page	Review the Faith at Home page. Encourage children to share this page at home.	**Act** Suggested activities for the home	PROGRAM RESOURCES Family Guide, pp. 30–31

CELEBRATE

Objective

To experience a celebration of the word, including a Blessing for Mission

Preparation

Familiarize yourself with the movements of the ritual for the Blessing for Mission on page 73.

Prepare the prayer space ahead of time. You will need:

- a Bible
- a table covered with a white cloth
- a candle and a large glass bowl filled with water on the prayer table

 Use the *Songs of Celebration* CD, track 14, to rehearse the suggested song, "Lead Us to the Water," or see one of the optional music suggestions on page 73.

Select a child to carry the Bible in procession.

We Gather

Invite children to assemble with their books.

Gather children into the prayer space with a procession.

- Have children follow you and the child carrying the Bible, as you lead the procession.

 As you process, lead children in singing using the *Songs of Celebration* CD, track 14.

- When all are assembled, light the prayer candle.
- Begin prayer, and lead the children in the Sign of the Cross.

Follow the order of prayer on pages 72–73.

We Listen

For the proclamation of the Gospel, you may use a Bible or the adapted reading in the *Child's Book* on pages 74–75.

CELEBRATE

We Gather

Procession

As you sing, walk forward slowly. Follow the person carrying the Bible.

Sing together.

Go now, love each other.
Thanks be to God.
We will be your spirit.
We will be your peace.
Let us love each other.
Lead us to the feast.

© 1998 Tom Kendzia, OCP

Leader: Let us pray.

Make the Sign of the Cross together.

We Listen

Leader: Loving God, open our hearts to the Holy Spirit as we listen to your word. We ask this through Jesus Christ our Lord.

All: Amen.

Leader: A reading from the Acts of the Apostles.

Read Acts 2:1–41.

The word of the Lord.

All: Thanks be to God.

Sit silently.

72

✦ Liturgical Background

Rite of Dismissal The word Mass is taken from some of the last words of the liturgy in Latin: *Ite, missa est.* In English these words for the dismissal of the assembly are translated: "Go, the Mass is ended." The word *missa,* from which the English word Mass comes, means "sent."

When people hear the words "Go in peace," they may think this means only that the celebration has ended. In fact, these simple words remind us that being Catholic means not only being called, but also being sent. Nourished by the Eucharist, we go forth to praise and serve God in the circumstances of our daily lives.

Ritual Focus: Blessing for Mission

Come forward, and gather around the holy water.

Leader: Just as the disciples were filled with the Holy Spirit and told the good news in word and action, so are we. Let us pray for God's blessing.

Lord Jesus, you came on earth to serve others. May your example strengthen us.

All: Amen.

Leader: Through your dying and rising, you made a new world where we are called to love one another. May we live according to your Gospel.

All: Amen.

Leader: Let us pray that God, who is love, will light our hearts with the fire of the Holy Spirit.

Bow your heads, and pray for God's blessing.

Blessed are you, God of mercy. Through your Son Jesus, you gave us an example of love. Send down your blessing on your children. Let them serve you in their neighbor.

All: Amen.

ADAPTED FROM THE BOOK OF BLESSINGS, 587

We Go Forth

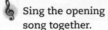

Make the Sign of the Cross with the water.

Leader: Go forth now to love and serve the Lord.

All: Thanks be to God.

 Sing the opening song together.

73

✳ Ritual Background

Blessing   A blessing has two aspects: the calling down of God's gifts and thanksgiving returned to God. When we bow to receive a blessing, we express an attitude of humility before God. But there is also a spirit of gratitude that rises up within us in response to God's blessing. Thus, with the psalmist we can say:

"Bless the LORD, my soul;
   all my being, bless his holy name!"

(Psalm 103:1)

The *Catechism* teaches that every baptized person is called to be a blessing and to bless *(CCC 1669)*. So, parents may bless

their children, lay catechists may bless catechumens, and so on. At Mass, however, it is only the priest who blesses the assembly. The blessing may be a simple invocation of the Trinity. On some occasions, a more solemn blessing may be used. To each of the invocations, the people respond, "Amen."

Ritual Focus: Blessing for Mission

- Invite children to stand and gather around the holy water.

- Raise your right hand as you pray the blessing.

We Go Forth

- Invite children to come forward individually and bless themselves.

- When all have blessed themselves, lead the closing prayer.

- As children return to their seats, have them sing *Songs of Celebration* CD, track 14, "Lead Us to the Water," or one of the optional music suggestions.

♪ **Optional Music Suggestions:**

"Id y enseñad/Go and Teach," © Gabarain. Published by OCP

"Eat This Bread," Les Presses de Taize. © GIA Publications

Objective

To explore the meaning of the ritual action of Blessing for Mission

To teach that we are sent forth from Mass to carry God's love to others

Liturgical Catechesis

The purpose of this section is to help children reflect on their experiences of the signs, rituals, prayers, and gestures of the celebration and to lead them to express their own meaning of the experiences. Allow children to share their experiences without commenting on them.

Being Blessed

- On the board or on chart paper, write the following questions: What did you see? What did you hear? What did you do?

- Guide children to reflect on the celebration by reviewing what happened in the prayer.

- Invite children to share their responses to the questions.

Reflect

- Invite children to complete the phrases with their own thoughts and feelings.

- Remind them that they do not have to respond to all the statements.

Blessing

- Read aloud the text.

- Discuss the different kinds of blessing.

Being Blessed

SIGNS OF FAITH

Blessing

A blessing is an action, using words and gestures, to ask God to show his kindness to us. There are many kinds of blessings. The Church blesses people and objects. Parents are blessed when their children are baptized. Animals are blessed on the feast of Saint Francis. Parents bless children at night or when they wake in the morning. The priest blesses special objects such as rosaries. At Mass the priest blesses the assembly.

74

Reflect

Blessing for a mission Think and write about the celebration.

When I receive a blessing

_____

_____

The Holy Spirit helps me

_____

_____

_____

When I serve people in need

_____

_____

_____

Additional Activity

Draw a picture Help children remember some of the phrases from the blessing you led during the celebration. Remind them that we are called to serve others.

- Distribute art materials.

- Have children draw a picture of one way they can serve others at home or school.

- Invite volunteers to share their pictures.

Sent on a Mission

Have you ever been sent to do a special job? Being sent means you are trusted. You represent someone else. You are responsible. Someone is counting on you. Without you, the job will not get done.

At the end of Mass, we are sent to carry the message of God's love to others. We are sent to help carry out the work of Jesus in the world. The word *Mass* comes from a word that means "to be sent on a mission." Receiving Jesus in Holy Communion strengthens us to love and serve others. We go out from Mass with God's blessing.

Witness

At tho ond of Mass, we are sent forth to be witnesses of faith in Jesus' presence in the world today. A witness is somebody who sees or hears something and tells others about it. We witness to Jesus' presence when we tell others about him in our words and in our actions.

75

Sent on a Mission

- Summarize the first paragraph, and have children share their experiences of being sent to do a special job.

- Have five volunteers each read aloud a sentence in the second paragraph.

- Encourage children to share their ideas about how they can carry God's love to others.

✝ Witness

- Summarize the text for children.

- Share one or two examples of people who are everyday witnesses of faith to you.

- Invite children to think of their own examples and share them.

💡 Teaching Tip

Use ordinary experiences When relating experiences or stories of people who are witnesses of faith or when giving examples of possibilities for mission, use experiences and examples children can relate to and possibly imitate. Otherwise, they may feel that acting for mission is not possible for them.

At the same time, be sure to use some examples that challenge children to think beyond the communities of family and school. You may be able to find these

kinds of examples in newspaper stories of individual children or groups of children who have reached out to others.

If possible, invite a representative from a parish organization or committee that is involved in outreach or social concerns activities. Ask him or her to present some ideas to the group that would be possible activities for children or families to be involved in.

Objective

To explain that the Holy Spirit is in our lives today

Faith Focus

What happens when we receive the Holy Spirit?
List children's responses on the board or on chart paper.

The Holy Spirit

Remind children that they pray to the Holy Spirit whenever they pray the Sign of the Cross. Recall that the Holy Spirit comes to us in a special way in the Sacraments of Initiation.

- Summarize the first paragraph of text to show children that Jesus sent the Holy Spirit to guide us.

- Emphasize that the Holy Spirit guides us in our mission to teach about God.

 Scripture ACTS 2:1–41

Pentecost

- Gather children into a story circle or in the prayer space. Remind them that they will be hearing the reading from the Acts of the Apostles again.

- Ask what they remember from hearing the reading during the celebration.

- Reread the scripture story aloud.

- Or, select some children to dramatize the story. Use the text on pages CE21–22 of this edition.

REMEMBER

The Holy Spirit

Faith Focus

What happens when we receive the Holy Spirit?

Before Jesus returned to his Father in heaven, he gave his disciples a mission. He wanted them to teach others about his message. Jesus promised the disciples he would send the Holy Spirit to help them with their mission. Fifty days after Jesus' Resurrection, his promise came true.

 Scripture

ACTS 2:1–41

Pentecost

During the feast of Pentecost, the disciples were all in one place together. Suddenly there came from the sky a noise like a strong wind. It filled the whole house. Then flames of fire came to rest above each of the disciples' heads. The disciples were filled with the Holy Spirit. They went out into the street and began to tell the crowd about Jesus and his message. The people who listened were surprised because the disciples were speaking in different languages. They wondered if something was wrong with the disciples!

76

Scripture Background

Beginnings Prior to the Christian Pentecost, the Jewish disciples of Jesus were quite small in number. The Acts of the Apostles tells us that they numbered only 120 (See *Acts 1:15*). When the Holy Spirit descended upon the followers of Jesus on Pentecost, they were transformed. They realized their mission was to preach the message of Jesus.

Although the Jewish people who had assembled for the Jewish feast of Pentecost were from different places and spoke different languages and dialects, they understood what the disciples were saying as they began to preach.

After Peter spoke to the large crowd, 3,000 people were added to the number of believers *(Acts 2:41)*. Empowered by this event, the Church spread to the Gentile world and grew rapidly.

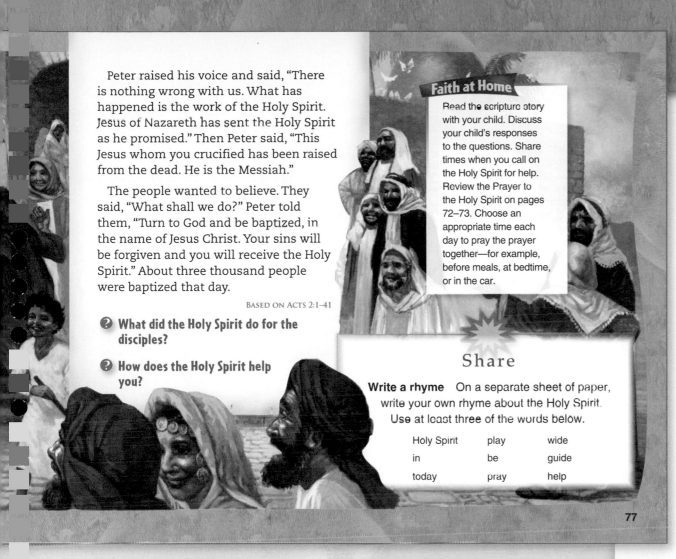

Peter raised his voice and said, "There is nothing wrong with us. What has happened is the work of the Holy Spirit. Jesus of Nazareth has sent the Holy Spirit as he promised." Then Peter said, "This Jesus whom you crucified has been raised from the dead. He is the Messiah."

The people wanted to believe. They said, "What shall we do?" Peter told them, "Turn to God and be baptized, in the name of Jesus Christ. Your sins will be forgiven and you will receive the Holy Spirit." About three thousand people were baptized that day.

BASED ON ACTS 2:1–41

? **What did the Holy Spirit do for the disciples?**

? **How does the Holy Spirit help you?**

Faith at Home

Read the scripture story with your child. Discuss your child's responses to the questions. Share times when you call on the Holy Spirit for help. Review the Prayer to the Holy Spirit on pages 72–73. Choose an appropriate time each day to pray the prayer together—for example, before meals, at bedtime, or in the car.

Share

Write a rhyme On a separate sheet of paper, write your own rhyme about the Holy Spirit. Use at least three of the words below.

Holy Spirit	play	wide
in	be	guide
today	pray	help

77

- Ask children what Peter said people should do. They should be baptized in the name of Jesus.

- Ask what happens after someone is baptized. They become members of the Church, their sins are forgiven, and they receive the Holy Spirit.

? Discuss the question. gave them courage, helped them speak in another language

? Discuss the question. Accept all reasonable responses.

Share

- Have children work alone or in small groups for the activity.

- Explain the activity to children, and set a time limit.

- Consider writing a rhyme as a class to model the activity.

- Have volunteers share their work.

Cultural Background

Pentecost Pentecost is a Greek word meaning "fifty." Sometimes referred to as the Feast of Weeks, this Jewish Feast of Pentecost (Exodus 34:22) celebrated the end of seven weeks of the cereal harvest. It was a major feast for which the Jewish people would travel from their homes to Jerusalem to make offerings at the Temple. This is probably why there were so many people of diverse languages and dialects in Jerusalem when Peter preached.

The descent of the Holy Spirit at the time of the Jewish Feast of Pentecost gave the feast new meaning for the Christians. The Jewish Feast of Pentecost provided a ready-made opportunity for the early Church to celebrate the descent of the Holy Spirit upon the first Christian community.

Review

- Jesus sent the Holy Spirit to help us teach about God the Father.

- The Holy Spirit came to the disciples on Pentecost.

Objective

To explain why we are sent forth from Mass

Faith Focus

How do we love and serve Jesus?

List children's responses on the board or on chart paper.

We Are Sent

Recall that Jesus sent his followers out on a mission. Tell children that every time we leave Mass, we are also sent on a mission.

- Have children read the bulleted text aloud.

- Talk about specific tasks that the Holy Spirit can help us with.

✠ Deacon

- Read aloud the text.

- If your parish has a deacon, tell children his name. Consider inviting him to your class to talk about his duties.

We Are Sent

REMEMBER

SIGNS OF FAITH

✠ **Deacon**

A **deacon** is a man ordained by the bishop to do the works of charity and to have a special role in worship. Some deacons become priests. Other deacons do not, but they help the bishop and care for people who need it. All deacons can baptize and witness a marriage. At Mass deacons may carry the Book of the Gospels, read the Gospel, and preach. They can also send us forth for mission at the end of Mass.

Faith Focus

How do we love and serve Jesus?

Like Peter and the disciples, Jesus promises us the Holy Spirit. The Holy Spirit is with us always. The Holy Spirit helps us:

- tell others about his love

- do the work of being a disciple

- forgive others

- care about people who need help, especially those who are poor

78

✦ Catechist Background

The experience of sacraments

Today the *Rite of Christian Initiation of Adults* is the model for all catechesis, and especially catechetical preparation for the Sacraments of Initiation. The rite restored the catechumenate as the norm for how unbaptized adults and children of catechetical age are to be made members of the Church.

It is interesting to note that in many catechumenates of the fourth and fifth centuries, persons who were being initiated did not receive complete instruction about the sacraments until after they had

experienced them. This practice contains an important lesson for today—namely, that the experience of the celebration of sacraments and reflection on that experience deepens a person's understanding of their meaning. Encourage children to celebrate the Eucharist often.

Go Forth

At the end of Mass, we are sent forth to serve others. The priest or deacon says, "Go in peace to love and serve the Lord." We respond, "Thanks be to God." We go forth to share the joyful good news that Jesus is alive. We share the good news by what we say and what we do.

When we leave the church after Mass, we are different from when we came in. Participating in the Eucharist changes us. It brings us closer to God the Father, Son, and Holy Spirit. It also brings us closer to one another.

In the Eucharist we become one body, just as many grains of wheat make one loaf of bread. We are filled with God's grace and love. We go forth to serve others. We go forth to help those who need our help. We love and serve Jesus when we love and serve one another.

❓ What are some ways your family helps others?

79

![star] **Sacrament Background**

Deacons   According to the oldest practices of the Catholic Church, the ministry of deacons as we know it today originated in the story found in *Acts 6:1–6*. The diaconate arose out of an expressed need articulated by the community of the Hellenistic Jews, who complained to the Apostles that their widows were being neglected.

The Apostles discerned that they could not leave their own service of the word and instead established the ministry of the diaconate for service to the widows. Stephen, who was also the first martyr, was one of the first deacons.

Go Forth

Recall that during the Mass we hear God's message in the Liturgy of the Word and receive Holy Communion during the Liturgy of the Eucharist.

- Summarize the first paragraph, and have children repeat the dismissal responses after you.

- Have children read the second paragraph, and discuss how we are different after we attend Mass. We are closer to God and to one another.

- Read the last paragraph aloud.

- Have children link the photographs with ideas in the text.

❓ Elicit answers to the question. Accept all reasonable responses.

Activity Master

You may wish to use Activity Master 8 on page CE20 to clarify the roles of bishops, priests, deacons, and extraordinary ministers.

▲ Activity Master 8

Review

- The Holy Spirit helps us serve others.

- When Mass ends, we are sent out to serve God and others.

Objective

To reinforce the concept of service

Sent to Serve

Respond

Explain the activity to children. Brainstorm story ideas with children.

- Help children organize their stories.
- Invite volunteers to share their stories with the class.

Closing Blessing

- Gather children into a prayer circle with their books.
- Begin with the Sign of the Cross.
- Read the People of Faith story of Saint Therese of Lisieux.
- Pray the prayer.

 End with the *Songs of Celebration* CD, track 14, "Lead Us to the Water," or one of the optional music suggestions on page 73.

Sent to Serve

Respond

Write a story Write a story about how you can serve others.

_____

_____

_____

_____

_____

_____

_____

_____

Closing Blessing

Gather and begin with the Sign of the Cross.

Leader: God, our Father, send us forth to tell the world about your love.

All: Amen.

Leader: Jesus, our Savior, send us forth to serve others.

All: Amen.

Leader: Holy Spirit, guide us to see the places where we are called to love and serve.

All: Amen.

Sing together.

Go now, love each other.
Thanks be to God.
We will be your spirit.
We will be your peace.
Let us love each other.
Lead us to the feast.

© 1998 Tom Kendzia, OCP

80

People of Faith: A Read Aloud Story

Saint Therese of Lisieux Therese was the youngest of five daughters. She lived in France. She loved Jesus very much and wanted to serve God as a missionary, but she was not strong enough. At fifteen, Therese became a Carmelite sister. She decided that the best thing she could do for others was to do the ordinary everyday things very well. She became known for her goodness. She wrote a book about her friendship with God. She only lived twenty-four years, but millions of people have read the book she wrote. Many of them learned to serve God by following Therese's example. After she died, the pope named her patroness of the missions.

C. 1873–1897

Faith at Home

Faith Focus

- The Eucharist changes us.
- The Holy Spirit helps us to live out our mission.
- At Mass we are sent forth to love and serve others.

Ritual Focus

Blessing for Mission The celebration focused on being sent forth for mission. The children were blessed and sent forth. Establish a family ritual of blessing each other with the Sign of the Cross on the forehead when you leave the house in the morning.

www.harcourtreligion.com
Visit our Web site for weekly scripture readings and questions, family resources, and more activities.

Act

Share Together Make a list of ways members of your family show love and care for each other. Then brainstorm together other ways the family might continue to show love and care. Suggest a family "love and serve" week. Write the names of family members on separate slips of paper. Have each member draw a name. Invite family members to do some "love and serve" actions for that person.

Do Together Obtain copies of the parish bulletin or newsletter. As a family, go through it and locate parish activities of service and outreach. Choose one that the whole family can get involved in, and call the parish to volunteer. After volunteering, hold a family discussion about the experience and how it felt to love and serve others.

Love and Serve Week

Family Prayer

Come Holy Spirit, show us the way and give us the strength to love and serve others. Amen.

81

Faith at Home

Review the five parts of the Faith at Home page with children.

Encourage children:

- to ask family members to review the Faith Focus statements
- to share the **Ritual Focus: Blessing for Mission** with family members
- to do at least one of the ☀ Act activities with family members
- to pray the Family Prayer with their family at times when the family is together
- to encourage their family members go to **www.harcourtreligion.com** with them and do the activities for this chapter sometime during the week

Words of Faith

Words of Faith

altar The table of the Eucharist. The Liturgy of the Eucharist is celebrated at the altar.

altar server A person who helps the priest and deacon at Mass.

ambo The reading stand from which the Scriptures are proclaimed. It is sometimes called the lectern.

assembly The baptized community gathered to celebrate the Eucharist, the sacraments, or other liturgy.

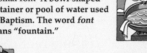

Baptism One of the three Sacraments of Initiation. Baptism gives us new life in God and makes us members of the Church.

baptismal font A bowl-shaped container or pool of water used for Baptism. The word *font* means "fountain."

Bible God's word written in human words. The Bible is the holy book of the Church.

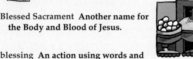

Blessed Sacrament Another name for the Body and Blood of Jesus.

blessing An action using words and gestures which asks God to show his kindness to us.

Body of Christ A name for the Church. It tells us that Christ is the head and the baptized are the members of the body.

Book of the Gospels A decorated book containing the readings from the four Gospels used during the Liturgy of the Word.

cantor The leader of song during the Mass and other Church celebrations.

chalice The special silver or gold cup used at Mass to hold the wine that becomes the Blood of Christ.

chrism The oil blessed by the bishop used in the Sacraments of Baptism, Confirmation, and Holy Orders.

Christian The name given to people who are baptized and follow Jesus.

Church The community of all baptized people who believe in God and follow Jesus.

ciborium The special silver or gold container used at Mass to hold the smaller consecrated Hosts for communion. A covered ciborium also holds the Blessed Sacrament in the tabernacle.

collection The gifts of money collected from members of the assembly and presented during the time of the Preparation of the Altar.

Confirmation One of the three Sacraments of Initiation. It is the sacrament that strengthens the life of God we received at Baptism and seals us with the gift of the Holy Spirit.

Confiteor A prayer of sorrow for sin. In it each person tells God and the Church family, "I am sorry." We ask for forgiveness.

82

83

Here are some suggested uses for these pages:

This section gives children a visual reference for the people, places, and things associated with the Eucharistic celebration. It contains some of the important words of faith used by the Church to help us understand the mystery of the Eucharist. Learning these words and their meanings will help children develop a Catholic vocabulary.

▶ Have children refer to these pages as the highlighted words of faith appear in each lesson. Have volunteers read the definitions aloud. Have children use each word in a sentence.

GO ONLINE Visit **www.harcourtreligion.com** for a downloadable black and white clip art of the illustrated Words of Faith.

consecration   The part of the Eucharistic Prayer when, through the prayers and actions of the priest and the power of the Holy Spirit, the gifts of bread and wine become the Body and Blood of Jesus.

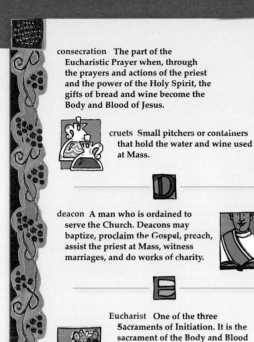

cruets   Small pitchers or containers that hold the water and wine used at Mass.

D

deacon   A man who is ordained to serve the Church. Deacons may baptize, proclaim the Gospel, preach, assist the priest at Mass, witness marriages, and do works of charity.

E

Eucharist   One of the three Sacraments of Initiation. It is the sacrament of the Body and Blood of Christ. Jesus is truly and really present in the Eucharist. The word *Eucharist* means "thanksgiving."

G

grace   A sharing in God's own life.

Holy Communion   The Body and Blood of Christ that we receive in the Eucharist.

Holy Trinity   The three Persons in one God: God the Father, God the Son, and God the Holy Spirit.

Host   A round piece of unleavened bread used at Mass. When the host is consecrated at Mass, it becomes the Body and Blood of Christ.

incense   Oils and spices that are burned in liturgical celebrations to show honor for holy things. It is also used as a sign of our prayers rising to God.

L

Lamb of God   A title for Jesus that reminds us that he offered his life through suffering and death to take away our sins.

 lectionary   The book of scripture readings used at Mass.

 lector   A person who proclaims God's word at Mass or other liturgical celebrations. The word *lector* means "reader."

Liturgy of the Eucharist   The second main part of the Mass. It is the time when we call on the Holy Spirit and the priest consecrates the bread and wine. We remember and give thanks for all of God's gifts, especially Jesus' life, death, and Resurrection.

Liturgy of the Word   The first main part of the Mass. It is the time when we listen to God's word in the Scriptures.

M

Mass   Another name for the Eucharist.

memorial   Another word for remembering. In the Mass, it means to remember and proclaim God's works.

mission   A job or duty someone is sent to do and takes responsibility for. The Church's mission is to announce the good news of God's kingdom.

mystery   Something we believe about God and his actions, but we do not understand how it happens.

O

original sin   The first sin committed by the first humans.

84

85

▶ As these words come up in the lessons, have children make their own set of Words of Faith vocabulary cards. Use index cards. Have children write the word on one side and the definition on the other side. They could also use these cards for a vocabulary word game, either in the session, while they are waiting for the session to begin, or at home with family members.

▶ Refer to these pages throughout the sessions to help children associate liturgical names with the objects, rituals, and people they describe.

▶ Invite children to draw their own illustrations for each of the terms.

Paschal candle Another name for the Easter Candle that is lit at the Easter Vigil.

paten The silver or gold plate or dish used at Mass to hold the large host.

Pentecost The feast that celebrates the coming of the Holy Spirit on the Apostles and disciples fifty days after Easter. We celebrate this day as the beginning of the Church.

People of God A name for the Church which tells us that we are sent by Christ to preach God's love to all people.

prayer Talking and listening to God. It is raising our minds and hearts to God.

preparation of the altar and gifts The part of the Mass when the altar is prepared and members of the assembly bring the bread and wine, which will become the Body and Blood of Jesus, to the priest at the altar.

priest A man who is ordained to serve God and lead the Church by celebrating the sacraments, preaching and presiding at Mass, and performing other spiritual works.

procession A group of people moving forward as part of a celebration.

sacrament A holy sign that comes from Jesus, which gives us a share in God's life.

sacramentary The book containing the Order of the Mass, special celebrations during the year, and various prayers used by the priest at Mass.

Sacraments of Initiation The three Sacraments of Baptism, Confirmation, and Holy Eucharist that together make us full members of the Church. They are signs that we belong to God and to the Catholic Church.

sanctuary The part of the church where the altar and ambo are located. The word *sanctuary* means "holy place."

Sign of Peace The sign of peace is an action prayer that we exchange before Communion as a sign to wish God's peace on those who receive it. It shows that we are one in Christ's love.

tabernacle The container in which the Blessed Sacrament is kept. It may be located in the sanctuary or a special chapel in the church. A lamp or candle is kept burning near the tabernacle as a sign that Jesus is present. The word *tabernacle* means "meeting place."

unity A word that means to be one with others.

usher A person of hospitality who welcomes members of the assembly to Mass and helps direct processions and collections.

vestments The special clothing worn by the priest and some others for Mass and other liturgical celebrations.

86

87

▶ If possible, take children on a tour of the church. Ask the sacristan or a parish minister to show children some of the sacred vessels and vestments used by your parish community. Have children note how what they see in the parish church is the same or different from the pictures in the book.

▶ At the end of the eight sessions, go through the Words of Faith glossary word by word and ask children to tell what each word means.

Order of the Mass

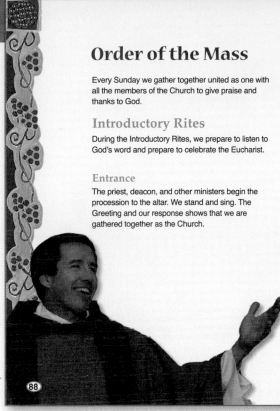

Order of the Mass

Every Sunday we gather together united as one with all the members of the Church to give praise and thanks to God.

Introductory Rites

During the Introductory Rites, we prepare to listen to God's word and prepare to celebrate the Eucharist.

Entrance

The priest, deacon, and other ministers begin the procession to the altar. We stand and sing. The Greeting and our response shows that we are gathered together as the Church.

Greeting of the Altar and the People

When the procession reaches the altar, the priest, deacon, and other ministers make a profound bow. The priest and deacon also kiss the altar as a sign of reverence. At special times the priest will burn incense at the cross and altar. The priest goes to his chair and leads us in the Sign of the Cross and Greeting.

Priest: In the name of the Father, and of the Son, and of the Holy Spirit.
People: Amen.
Priest: The grace and peace of God our Father and the Lord Jesus Christ be with you.
People: And also with you.

Rite of Sprinkling with Holy Water

On some Sundays, the priest does a Rite of Sprinkling in place of the Penitential Rite. We are blessed with holy water to remind us of our Baptism.

Penitential Rite

The priest invites the assembly to confess our sins together.

Confiteor

I confess to Almighty God
and to you, my brothers and sisters,
that I have sinned through my own fault,
in my thoughts and in my words,
in what I have done,
and in what I have failed to do;
and I ask Blessed Mary ever virgin,
all the angels and saints,
and you, my brothers and sisters,
to pray for me to the Lord our God.

Lord Have Mercy

Priest: Lord, have mercy.
People: Lord, have mercy.
Priest: Christ, have mercy.
People: Christ, have mercy.
Priest: Lord, have mercy.
People: Lord, have mercy.
Priest: May almighty God have mercy on us, forgive us our sins, and bring us to everlasting life.
People: Amen.

Gloria

On some Sundays, we praise God the Father, the Son, and the Holy Spirit.

Glory to God in the highest,
    and peace to his people on earth.
Lord God, heavenly King,
almighty God and Father,
    we worship you, we give you thanks,
    we praise you for your glory.
Lord Jesus Christ, only Son of the Father,
Lord God, Lamb of God,
you take away the sin of the world:
    have mercy on us;
you are seated at the right hand of the Father:
    receive our prayer.
For you alone are the Holy One,
you alone are the Lord,
you alone are the Most High,
    Jesus Christ,
    with the Holy Spirit,
    in the glory of God the Father. Amen.

88

89

Use the Order of the Mass on pages 88–99 of the *Child's Book* to help children learn the parts of the Mass. The Order of the Mass includes the prayers and responses used during the Mass.

Here are some suggested uses for these pages:

● ● ● ● ● ● ● ● ● ▶

▶ At the end of the first session, invite children to turn to these pages. Explain that during the next seven sessions they will be learning different parts of the Mass. Do a general review of the Order of the Mass with children. Use the headings and pictures to review. This will also help you know what children already know about the Mass.

▶ Direct children's attention to these pages and encourage them to go through the pages with family members at home.

▶ Refer to the appropriate sections of the Order of the Mass as you teach each lesson:

Lesson 2 Introductory Rites and Gloria

Lesson 3 Penitential Rite

Lesson 4 Liturgy of the Word

Lesson 5 Liturgy of the Eucharist: Preparation of the Gifts

Lesson 6 Liturgy of the Eucharist: Eucharistic Prayer

Lesson 7 Liturgy of the Eucharist: Communion Rite

Lesson 8 Concluding Rite: Dismissal

Collect

The priest invites us to pray. We are silent for a moment and remember we are in God's presence. We think about what we want to pray for.

Priest: Let us pray...
People: Amen.

Liturgy of the Word

The Liturgy of the Word is celebrated at every Mass. We listen to God's word in the Readings and Homily, and we respond to God's word in the Creed and Prayers of the Faithful. The lectors and the priest or deacon read the readings from the ambo.

First Reading

We sit and listen to God's word from the Old Testament or the Acts of the Apostles. At the end of the reading, we respond:

Reader: The word of the Lord.
People: Thanks be to God.

Responsorial Psalm

At the end of the first reading, the cantor, or song leader, leads us in singing a psalm from the Old Testament.

People: Sing or say the refrain.

Second Reading

We listen to God's word from the New Testament books that are not Gospels. At the end of the reading, we respond:

Reader: The word of the Lord.
People: Thanks be to God.

Acclamation Before the Gospel

We stand and welcome the Lord, who speaks to us in the Gospel reading. We sing an Alleluia or another acclamation to profess our faith in God's presence.

People: Sing or say the Alleluia or Gospel Acclamation.

Gospel

Priest or deacon: The Lord be with you.
People: And also with you.
Priest or deacon: A reading from the holy Gospel according to...
People: Glory to you, Lord.

The priest and people make the Sign of the Cross on the forehead, lips, and heart.

At the end of the Gospel, we respond:

Priest or deacon: The Gospel of the Lord.
People: Praise to you, Lord Jesus Christ.

Homily

We sit and listen. The priest or deacon helps us understand the word of God. He shows us how we can live as Jesus' disciples.

Profession of Faith

We stand and respond to the readings by saying the Creed. We profess our faith in God the Father, God the Son, and God the Holy Spirit. We pray the Nicene Creed or the Apostles' Creed.
(For Nicene Creed, see page 92. For Apostles' Creed, see page 102.)

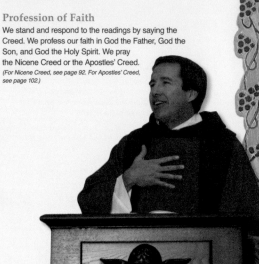

Here are some suggested uses for these pages:

▶ Review the parts of the Liturgy of the Word. Go over the different postures during this part of the Mass. Be sure children know when to sit and when to stand.

▶ Read the Nicene Creed on page 92 with children. Point out where the Persons of the Blessed Trinity are mentioned. Have children read the Creed aloud.

▶ Have children look at the Apostles' Creed on page 102. Point out that the Apostles' Creed is shorter than the Nicene Creed but also contains statements about what we believe.

Nicene Creed

People: We believe in one God, the Father,
the Almighty,
maker of heaven and earth,
of all that is seen and unseen.
We believe in one Lord,
Jesus Christ,
the only Son of God,
eternally begotten of the Father,
God from God, Light from Light,
true God from true God,
begotten, not made, one in Being
with the Father.
Through him all things
were made.
For us men and for our salvation
he came down from heaven:
by the power of the Holy Spirit
he was born of the Virgin Mary,
and became man.
For our sake he was crucified under
Pontius Pilate;
he suffered, died, and was buried.

On the third day he rose
again in fulfillment of
the Scriptures;
he ascended into heaven and is
seated at the right hand of
the Father.
He will come again in glory
to judge the living and the dead,
and his kingdom will have
no end.
We believe in the Holy Spirit, the
Lord, the giver of life,
who proceeds from the Father
and the Son.
With the Father and the Son he is
worshiped and glorified.
He has spoken through the
Prophets.
We believe in one holy
catholic and apostolic Church.
We acknowledge one baptism for
the forgiveness of sins.
We look for the resurrection of the
dead, and the life of the world
to come.
Amen.

General Intercessions

We stand and the priest, deacon, or a layperson leads us in praying for the needs of the Church, the world, those who need our prayers, and our local community. We say or sing the response that the leader tells us to say or sing.

Liturgy of the Eucharist

During the Liturgy of the Eucharist, we bring our gifts of bread and wine to the altar. We give thanks to God the Father for all the ways he has saved us. Our gifts of bread and wine become the Body and Blood of Christ. We all receive the Lord's Body and the Lord's Blood in communion.

Preparation of the Gifts

We sit as the gifts of bread and wine are brought to the altar. The altar is prepared as the collection is taken up. Sometimes we sing a song during the preparation.

The priest lifts up the bread and prays:

Priest: Blessed are you, Lord God of all creation.
Through your goodness we have this bread to offer which earth has given and human hands have made. It will become for us the bread of life.

People: Blessed be God forever.

The priest lifts up the chalice of wine and prays:

Priest: Blessed are you, Lord
God of all creation.
Through your goodness we have
this wine to offer,
fruit of the vine and work
of human hands.
It will become our spiritual drink.

People: Blessed be God forever.

The priest calls us to pray.

Priest: Pray, my brothers and sisters,
that our sacrifice may be acceptable
to God, the almighty Father.

People: May the Lord accept the sacrifice
at your hands
for the praise and glory
of his name,
for our good,
and the good of all his Church.

▶ Explain the different groups we pray for in the General Intercessions. If you have time during the session, organize children into four groups and have each group write an intercession.

▶ Review the responses your parish usually prays in the General Intercessions.

Prayer over the Offerings

We stand and pray with the priest. We prepare for the Eucharistic Prayer.

People: Amen.

Eucharistic Prayer

This is the central prayer of the Eucharist. It is a prayer of thanksgiving and making holy.

Preface

The priest invites us to pray. We say or sing the preface.

Priest: The Lord be with you.
People: And also with you.
Priest: Lift up your hearts.
People: We lift them up to the Lord.
Priest: Let us give thanks to the Lord our God.
People: It is right to give him thanks and praise.

Acclamation

Together with the priest, we say or sing:

Holy, holy, holy Lord, God of power and might,
Heaven and earth are full of your glory.
Hosanna in the Highest.
Blessed is he who comes in the name of the Lord.
Hosanna in the highest.

The priest continues to pray the Eucharistic prayer. During the Eucharistic prayer the priest tells the story of all of God's saving actions.

Consecration

The priest takes the bread and says the words of Jesus:

Take this, all of you, and eat it:
this is my Body which will be given up for you.

The priest holds up the consecrated bread, the Host, which is now the Body of Christ.

Then the priest takes the chalice, the cup of wine, and says the words of Jesus:

Take this, all of you, and drink from it:
this is the cup of my Blood,
the Blood of the new and everlasting covenant.
It will be shed for you and for all
so that sins may be forgiven.
Do this in memory of me.

The bread and wine become the Body and Blood of Jesus through the power of the Holy Spirit and the words and actions of the priest. Jesus is truly present under the appearances of bread and wine. We proclaim our faith in Jesus.

Memorial Acclamation

Priest or deacon: Let us proclaim the mystery of faith.
People: Christ has died, Christ is risen, Christ will come again.

The priest continues the Eucharistic Prayer. He prays for the whole Church, those who are living and those who are dead. He ends the prayer by singing or saying aloud:

Priest: Through him, with him, in him, in the unity of the Holy Spirit, all glory and honor is yours, almighty Father, for ever and ever.
People: Amen.

▶ If possible, obtain permission to take children to the church. Have them bring their books. Have some children gather around the altar and others in the pews. Go through the actions of each part of the Mass from the presider's part and the assembly's responses.

▶ Have children note what is the same and what is different when comparing the photos in the book to their church.

▶ Point out that although there are differences in the building, vestments, or vessels used in their parish, the prayers, responses, and actions of the priest and the assembly during Mass are the same.

▶ Using these pages, go over all the acclamations and responses in this section with children. Role-play them with children taking turns being the presider.

▶ Practice the sung parts of the Eucharistic Prayer with children. If you are not musically inclined, invite one of the parish musicians to sing with children.

Communion Rite

We stand for the Lord's Prayer. We pray for our daily bread. We pray our sins will be forgiven.

Lord's Prayer

People: Our Father, who art in heaven,
hallowed be thy name;
thy kingdom come;
thy will be done on earth as it is in
heaven.
Give us this day our daily bread;
and forgive us our trespasses
as we forgive those who trespass
against us;
and lead us not into temptation,
But deliver us from evil.

Priest: Deliver us, Lord, from every evil...

People: For the kingdom, the power
and the glory are yours,
now and forever.

Sign of Peace

The priest or deacon invites us to share a Sign of Peace with those around us. We pray for peace and that the Church and the world will be united as one.

Priest: The peace of the Lord be with you
always.

People: And also with you.

We offer one another a sign of peace.

Breaking of the Bread

Just as Jesus broke bread at the Last Supper and gave it to his disciples, the priest breaks the consecrated bread and puts a piece of it into the chalice to show the unity of Jesus' Body and Blood. During the breaking of the bread, we say or sing:

People: Lamb of God, you take away the sins
of the world: have mercy on us.
Lamb of God, you take away the sins
of the world: have mercy on us.
Lamb of God, you take away the sins
of the world: grant us peace.

Communion

The priest shows us the consecrated bread. He holds the Host up and invites us to the banquet of the Lord. We respond:

People: Lord, I am not worthy
to receive you,
but only say the word and
I shall be healed.

The priest receives Holy Communion. We sing the Communion hymn. When it is time, we walk in procession to receive Holy Communion. The minister offers us the consecrated bread, the Body of Christ. We bow our heads as a sign of reverence before receiving the Body of Christ.

**Priest or extraordinary
minister:** The Body of Christ.

People: Amen.

96

97

▶ As a final preparation for the celebration of First Holy Communion, use the Order of the Mass to review all the prayers and responses.

▶ Show children how to pray the Lord's Prayer with arms and hands in the orans position. The orans position is one where the forearms are extended with palms of the hands facing up.

▶ Teach children a sung Lamb of God that is part of the parish repertoire. If you are not musically inclined, invite one of the parish musicians to sing with children.

We receive the Body of Christ in our hand or on our tongue. We reverently chew and swallow the consecrated bread.

If we are receiving the consecrated wine, the Blood of Christ, the minister offers us the cup. We bow our head as a sign of reverence before receiving the Blood of Christ.

Priest or extraordinary minister: The Blood of Christ.
People: Amen.

We return to our seats and give thanks for the wonderful gift of Jesus we have received in Communion.

When the distribution of Communion is finished, the priest and people pray privately. A song may be sung at this time.

Prayer After Communion

We stand. The priest invites us to pray with him as he asks God to help us live as God's People, the Body of Christ.

Priest: Let us pray…
People: Amen.

Concluding Rite

We stand for the concluding rite. The priest greets us, blesses us in the name of the Holy Trinity, and sends us forth to live as Jesus' disciples.

Greeting

Priest: The Lord be with you.
People: And also with you.

Blessing

Priest: May Almighty God bless you in the name of the Father, the Son, and the Holy Spirit.
People: Amen.

Dismissal

Priest: Go in peace to love and serve the Lord.
People: Thanks be to God.

We sing a hymn of praise. The priest kisses the altar as a sign of reverence. He and the other ministers leave in procession.

▶ Talk with children about the period of silence after Communion. Suggest that they use that time for prayer and reflection.

▶ Discuss why the priest reverences the altar by kissing it.

Receiving Communion

Holy Communion

Rules for Receiving Holy Communion

- Only baptized Catholics may receive Communion.

- To receive Holy Communion, we must be in the state of grace, free from mortal sin. If we have sinned mortally, we must first go to the Sacrament of Reconciliation and receive absolution before receiving Holy Communion. When we are sorry for our venial sins, receiving Holy Communion frees us from them.

- To honor the Lord, we fast for one hour before the time we receive Communion. This means we go without food or drink, except water or medicine.

- Catholics are required to receive Holy Communion at least once a year during Easter time. But we are encouraged to receive Communion every time we participate in the Mass.

How to Receive Communion

When we receive Jesus in Holy Communion, we welcome him by showing reverence. These steps can help you.

- Fold your hands, and join in the singing as you wait in line.

- When it is your turn, you can receive the Body of Christ in your hand or on your tongue.

- When you are shown the Eucharist, bow in reverence.

- To receive the Body of Christ in your hand, hold your hands out with the palms up. Place one hand underneath the other, and cup your hands slightly.

- To receive the Host on your tongue, fold your hands, open your mouth, and put your tongue out.

- The person who offers you Communion will say, "The Body of Christ." You say, "Amen." The priest, deacon, or extraordinary minister of Holy Communion places the Host in your hand or on your tongue. Step aside, and chew and swallow the host.

- You may choose to drink from the cup. When the cup is offered to you, the person will say, "The Blood of Christ." You say, "Amen." Take a small sip.

- Return to your place in church. Pray quietly in your own words. Thank Jesus for being with you.

Rules for Receiving Holy Communion

▶ Review these rules and regulations with children and encourage them to go over them with their parents.

▶ The rules for receiving Holy Communion are based on Canon Law, the official law of the Church. Be sure to point that the Church emphasizes the importance of receiving Holy Communion frequently.

▶ Explain to children that not all Christians share our belief in the real Presence of Jesus in the Eucharist. That is why only Roman Catholics may receive Holy Communion at Mass.

▶ Review the definitions of mortal and venial sin. Remind children that through reception of Holy Communion venial sins are forgiven.

How to Receive Communion

▶ Review the directions for receiving Communion as the time for the celebration draws near. Role-play receiving the Body and Blood of Jesus so children are comfortable and at ease. If possible, invite parish extraordinary ministers of Holy Communion to practice with children. If appropriate, use unconsecrated hosts and wine. Emphasize the importance of reverence in receiving Communion. Be sure to practice the bowing gesture.

▶ Provide any additional information about how Holy Communion is distributed in your parish, such as directions for coming forward and returning to one's place, standing and kneeling, and receiving Holy Communion in the hand or on the tongue.

Catholic Prayers

Catholic Prayers

Lord's Prayer

Our Father, who art in heaven,
hallowed be thy name;
thy kingdom come;
thy will be done on earth as it is in heaven.
Give us this day our daily bread;
and forgive us our trespasses
as we forgive those who trespass against us;
and lead us not into temptation,
but deliver us from evil.
Amen.

Apostles' Creed

I believe in God, the Father almighty,
creator of heaven and earth.
I believe in Jesus Christ, his only Son, our Lord.
He was conceived by the power of
    the Holy Spirit
and born of the Virgin Mary.
He suffered under Pontius Pilate,
was crucified, died, and was buried.
He descended to the dead.
On the third day he rose again.
He ascended into heaven,
and is seated at the right hand of the Father.
He will come again to judge the living
    and the dead.
I believe in the Holy Spirit,
the holy catholic Church,
the communion of saints,
the forgiveness of sins,
the resurrection of the body,
and the life everlasting.
Amen.

Nicene Creed

We believe in one God, the Father,
    the Almighty,
    maker of heaven and earth,
    of all that is seen and unseen.
We believe in one Lord,
    Jesus Christ,
    the only Son of God,
    eternally begotten of the Father,
    God from God, Light from Light,
    true God from true God,
    begotten, not made, one in Being
        with the Father.
    Through him all things were made.
For us men and for our salvation
    he came down from heaven:
by the power of the Holy Spirit
    he was born of the Virgin Mary,
    and became man.
For our sake he was crucified under
        Pontius Pilate;
    he suffered, died, and was buried.
On the third day he rose
    again in fulfillment of
    the Scriptures;

he ascended into heaven and is
    seated at the right hand of
    the Father.
He will come again in glory
    to judge the living and the dead,
and his kingdom will have
    no end.
We believe in the Holy Spirit, the
    Lord, the giver of life,
    who proceeds from the Father
    and the Son.
With the Father and the Son he is
    worshiped and glorified.
He has spoken through the
    Prophets.
We believe in one holy
    catholic and apostolic Church.
We acknowledge one baptism for
    the forgiveness of sins.
We look for the resurrection of the
    dead, and the life of the world
    to come.
Amen.

102

103

The Lord's Prayer

▶ Teach children a musical version of the Lord's Prayer. Choose a selection where the phrases of the prayer are echoed.

▶ Show children the orans posture used when the Lord's Prayer is prayed during the Eucharist. Remind children to join in praying or singing the Lord's Prayer during the Eucharist.

Apostles' Creed

▶ Tell children that the Apostles' Creed contains the truths taught by the Apostles.

▶ Point out that the Creed outlines Christian doctrine and our Catholic faith.

Nicene Creed

▶ Have children compare the Nicene Creed to the Apostles' Creed. Ask: What are the differences? What is the same?

Confiteor

I confess to Almighty God
and to you, my brothers and sisters,
that I have sinned through my own fault,
in my thoughts and in my words,
in what I have done,
and in what I have failed to do;
and I ask Blessed Mary ever virgin,
all the angels and saints,
and you, my brothers and sisters,
to pray for me to the Lord our God.

Gloria

Glory to God in the highest,
  and peace to his people on earth.
Lord God, heavenly King,
almighty God and Father,
  we worship you, we give you thanks,
  we praise you for your glory.
Lord Jesus Christ, only Son of the Father,
Lord God, Lamb of God,
you take away the sin of the world:
  have mercy on us;
you are seated at the right hand of the
Father:
  receive our prayer.
For you alone are the Holy One,
you alone are the Lord,
you alone are the Most High,
  Jesus Christ,
  with the Holy Spirit,
  in the glory of God the Father.
Amen.

Hail Mary

Hail, Mary, full of grace!
The Lord is with you!
Blessed are you among women,
and blessed is the fruit of your
  womb, Jesus.
Holy Mary, Mother of God,
pray for us sinners,
now and at the hour of our death.
Amen.

Come, Holy Spirit

Come, Holy Spirit, fill the hearts of your
  faithful
And kindle in them the fire of your love.
Send forth your Spirit and they shall be
  created.
And you shall renew the face of the earth.

Grace Before Meals

Bless us, O Lord, and these your gifts,
which we are about to receive
from your goodness.
Through Christ our Lord.
Amen.

Grace After Meals

We give you thanks for all your gifts,
almighty God,
living and reigning now and forever.
Amen.

Confiteor

▶ Explain to children that *Confiteor* means "I confess."

▶ Remind children that this prayer is sometimes used as part of the Penitential Rite at Mass.

▶ Go through each of the phrases of the Confiteor with children. Point out:
  • that the confession is to God and the community;
  • that sin includes commission and omission;
  • that we ask help from Mary, the angels and saints, and one another not to sin again.

▶ Explain to children that the Confiteor is an expression of sorrow for our sins during the Penitential Rite.

▶ Have children make prayer cards with the words of the Confiteor to use as a reminder when they celebrate Mass.

Gloria

▶ Point out that the Gloria can be said or sung at Mass.

▶ Tell children that the Gloria is sometimes called the "Angelic Hymn" because it is similar to the song the angels sang at Bethlehem in Luke 2:14. You may wish to read this passage aloud so children can hear the similarity.

Hail Mary

▶ Explain to children that the Hail Mary combines elements of the angel Gabriel's greeting (Luke 1:28) and Elizabeth's greeting (Luke 1:42) to Mary. You may wish to read these passages aloud so the children can hear the similarity to the words of the Hail Mary.

Come, Holy Spirit

▶ Encourage children to learn this prayer and to say it any time they want to call upon the Holy Spirit for help but especially before examining their consciences.

Grace Before and After Meals

▶ Encourage children to share these prayers with their families at mealtime.

Boldfaced numbers refer to pages on which the terms are defined in the Child's Book.

Alleluia, **38**
altar, **45**
ambo, **38**
Apostles' Creed, **102**
assembly, **14**

Baptism, 2, 3, 4, **5**, 11, 34
Bible, **35**, 41
Blessed Sacrament, **58**
blessing, **74**
Body and Blood of Jesus/Christ,
    9, **48**, 55, **58**, 59, 61, 93
Body of Christ, **5**, **21**, **101**
Book of the Gospels, **38**
Bread of Life, 65, 68, 71
bread and wine/Bread and Wine,
    48, 49, **58**, 69

chalice, **65**
chrism, **9**
Christ
    light of, 5
    new life in, 8
Christian(s), **5**, 16–17, 21
Church, **5**, **21**
ciborium, **65**
collection, **49**
Come, Holy Spirit, **105**
Communion Rite, 68, 96
community of faith, **16**, 18, 21
Confirmation, **9**, 11
Confiteor, 22, 24, **29**, 31, 89, **104**
consecration, **59**, 94
Creed, 39, 91
cross, 42, **44**, 45, 51
crucifix, **44**

deacon, **78**
disciples, **5**, 6, 34, 48, 56

Easter, 5
Eucharist, **9**, 11, **21**, 28, **31**, **48**, **65**,
    79, 81
Eucharistic Prayer, **55**, 58, 59, **61**, 94

general intercessions, **39**
Gloria, 12, 21, 89, **104**
God, 35
God's saving actions and
    promises, 61
God's word/word of God, 39, 41
good news, 35, 36, 38, 39, 79
Gospel(s), **36**, 38, 91
Grace After Meals, **105**
Grace Before Meals, **105**
Great Amen, **59**, **61**

Hail Mary, **105**
Holy Communion, 9, 65, 68, 69,
    71, 75, 100
holy oil of chrism, 9
Holy Spirit, 5, 8, 35, 48, 51, 55, 61,
    65, 78, 81
    gift of the, 9
Holy Trinity, **8**, 14
holy water, 28
homily, **39**, 91
Honoring the Cross, 42, 51
Host(s), 58, 69

Introductory Rites, **19**, **21**, 38, 88

Jesus, 6–7, 19, 35, 36–37, 48, 55,
    56–57, 58, 71, 75
    new life with, 5
    sacrifice of, 45, 51

kneeling, **54**

Lamb of God, **68**, 69
Last Supper, 55, **56**, 58, 59
lectionary, **38**
Liturgy of the Eucharist, **38**, 46,
    48, 49, 93
Liturgy of the Word, **38**, 39, 41, 90
Lord Have Mercy, **24**, 89
Lord's Prayer, 68, **102**

Mass, 9, 28, 35, 38, 45, 48, 51, **71**,
    75, 79, 81

Memorial Acclamation, 53, **59**, 61, 95
mission, 75, 81
mystery of faith, **55**

New Testament, **35**, 38
Nicene Creed, **92**, **103**

Old Testament, **35**, 38
Original sin, 5

Paschal Candle, **5**
Passover, 56–57
paten, **65**
Penitential Rite, **22**, 24, 28, 29, 31, 88
People of God, **21**, 31
prayer, **15**, 18
prayer of the faithful, **39**
Preparation of the Gifts, **49**, 93
priest, 19, **55**, 61
procession, 12, **15**, 21
psalm, **38**

readings, 38
renewal of baptismal promises, 2, 11

sacrament, **8**, **11**
Sacraments of Initiation, **8**, **11**
sacrifice(s), **45**, 48, 49, 51, 58
Scriptures, **35**
Sign of the Cross, **34**, 41
Sign of Peace, **23**, 43, **64**, 68, 96
silence, 15, **25**
sin, 31
singing, **18**
sower, the, 36–37
sprinkling with holy water, **28**, 88

tabernacle, **58**
Table of the Lord, 64

vine and the branches, 6–7

water, **4**
witness, **75**

CALL to CELEBRATE

EUCHARIST

Program Resources

Name _____

The Vine and the Branches

Finish the branches on this vine. Next to each branch, write the name of a person who belongs to God. Draw a picture of that person in the oval nearest to the name.

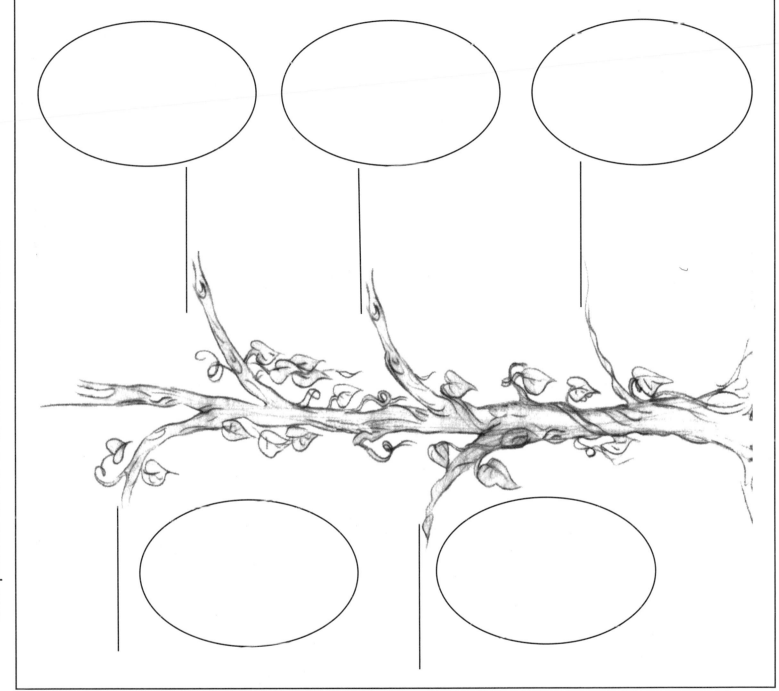

The Vine and the Branches

Based on John 15:1–17

Echo Pantomime

One day Jesus was talking to his friends.
(Flap thumb against fingers to indicate talking.)

He said: I am the true vine,
(Wiggle fingers upward like growing vine.)

And my Father takes care of the vine.
(Pat hands as if caressing vine.)

He cuts off the dead branches,
(Clipping motions with index and middle fingers.)

So that the good branches have even more fruit.
(Spread arms.)

You are the branches,
(Point to others.)

If you stay connected to me,
(Reach out and pull arms together in a hug.)

You will be a branch with lots of fruit.
(Make motions as if pulling apples off a tree.)

If you stay connected to me,
(Reach out and pull arms together in a hug.)

If you let my words come into your hearts,
(Place both hands over heart.)

Wonderful things will happen to you.
(Throw hands and arms open in surprise and wonderment.)

Just as the Father loves me; I love you.
(Reach out and pull arms together in a hug.)

If you do everything I've told you to do,
(Move hand several times in circle to indicate "everything.")

You will be very happy.
(Put a finger at each side of mouth and make a smiley face.)

And remember the most important thing I've told you to do:
(Tap forehead.)

Love one another just as I love you.
(Reach out and pull arms together as if in a hug.)

ACTIVITY MASTER 2

Name _____

The Early Christians

Decorate these wristbands, and cut them out. Wear one yourself. Give the others to members of your faith community.

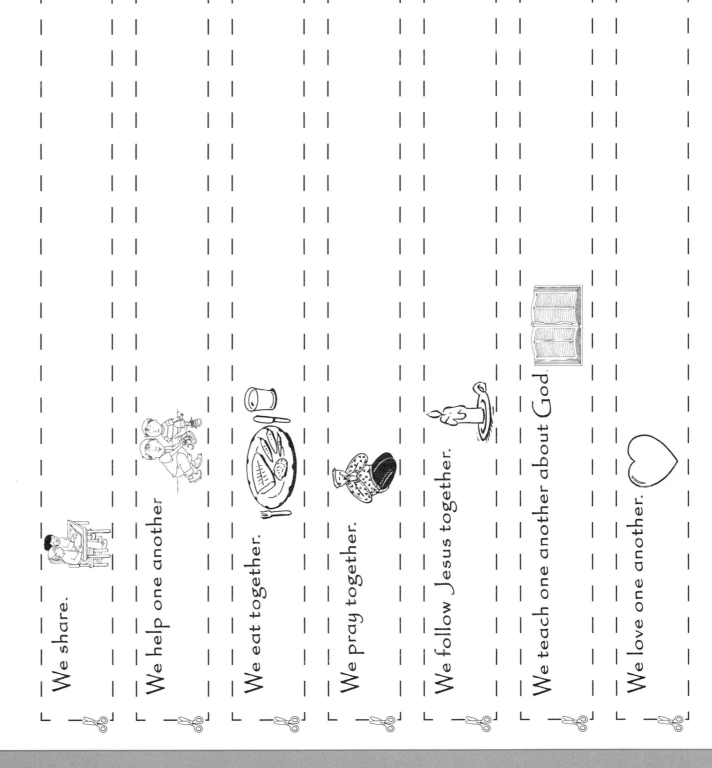

We share.

We help one another

We eat together.

We pray together.

We follow Jesus together.

We teach one another about God.

We love one another.

The Early Christians

Based on Acts 2:42–47

Overview

Props

Group 1 Table(s) or desks and chairs, refreshments

Group 2 Two or three name cards with the word APOSTLE printed on them. These can be made with poster paper and string or yarn so they can be placed around the children's necks.
Bandages, sunglasses, slings for those who will play the part of the sick people.
Bag with food to be distributed.

Group 3 None

Costume Ideas

Note: Costumes are not necessary but can add to the children's participation in and understanding of the Scriptures.

All characters may wear simple cloth or paper tunics with rope or yarn belts. Some may wear bathrobes as outerwear. Veils for women and headdresses for men may be improvised from pillowcases and towels. Performers may wear sandals or be barefoot.

Setting

Designate a different space in your session room for each of the three groups. If your space is limited, do the drama in three separate scenes in a place where all can see.

Preparation

Familiarize yourself with the drama on page CE5. Plan how to use the space where you hold your sessions for the drama. If you are going to use them, collect props and costumes. Select children for the cast.

Cast

Organize the class into three groups so that half the children are in Group 2. Then arrange the other half of the class in two groups. They will be Groups 1 and 3.

• Group 1 will form the scene of the Christians eating and praying together. Assign one child to distribute food to the group.

• Group 2 will form the scene of the sick and poor with the Apostles. Assign one or two children to distribute food.

• Group 3 will form the group of onlookers.

• Narrator

• Apostles (two or three)

• Speaker for Group 1

Give directions to each group and the cast.

Dramatization

Narrator: *(stands between Groups 1 and 2)*
The early Christians loved God. They loved each other. They listened carefully to the words of the Apostles. They ate special meals together where they prayed and broke bread and shared the cup. They took care of the sick and poor.

While the narrator is speaking, the scenes below are acted out at the same time:

• **Group 3:** Children gather together and observe Groups 1 and 2.

• **Group 2:** One or two children wear sunglasses or blinders. One child puts a bandage or sling on another child. Children who are Apostles move among them and put their hands on their heads and pray for them. One or two children distribute food to the poor.

• **Group 1:** Children sit at the table and one person distributes refreshments. Children begin to talk quietly.

• **Group 2:** When Group 1 begins to talk, the sick in Group 2 show signs of being healed (a child removes a bandage or sling from another; the child with blinders or sunglasses takes them off). The poor receive the food and say, "Thank you." Group 2 moves to the table.

When Group 2 is at the table, speaker turns to Group 3:

Group 1 Speaker: I want to tell you who we are. We are followers of Jesus. Jesus told us to love one another. We all live together and take care of one another.

Group 3: We can see how special your new life is! We want to know Jesus, too. Can we join you? Will you teach us about Jesus?

Group 1 Speaker: Yes, come with us and you can live a special life in Jesus too.

Some in the Group 3 crowd come to the table and are welcomed by Groups 1 and 2 at the table.

ACTIVITY MASTER 3

All Are Welcome!

Color in the drawing at the center of the page. Color the sides. Cut along the heavy lines, and fold along the dotted lines. Fold the sides toward the front. Your drawing can stand up on its own! If you like, you can decorate the outside of the side panels to look like church doors.

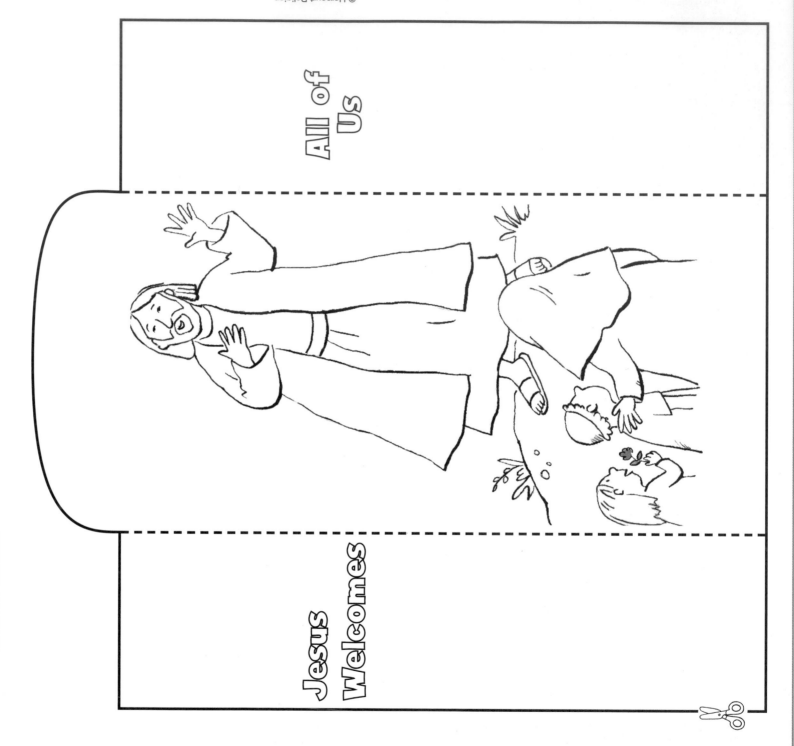

All of Us

Jesus Welcomes

The Call of Matthew

Based on Matthew 9:9–13

Overview

Props

Desk or table and chair
Play money on desk or table
Signs: *Matthew, Jesus, disciples* (two or three), *Pharisee*
Table with chairs
Refreshments

Costume Ideas

Note: Costumes are not necessary but can add to the children's participation in and understanding of the Scriptures.

All characters may wear simple cloth or paper tunics with rope or yarn belts. Some may wear bathrobes as outerwear. Veils for women and headdresses for men may be improvised from pillowcases and towels. Performers may wear sandals or be barefoot.

Setting

Designate two different spaces in your session room, one for the scene of Matthew at the tax collector's table and one for the meal at Matthew's house. If your space is limited, do the drama in two separate scenes in a place where all can see.

Preparation

Familiarize yourself with the drama on page CE8. Plan how to use the space where you do your sessions for the drama. If you are going to use them, collect props and costumes. Select children for the cast.

Cast

Organize the class into two groups:
• Group 1 will form the scene at the tax collector's table with Jesus and the disciples.
• Group 2 will form the scene of Matthew's friends.
• Jesus
• Matthew
• Disciples
• Pharisee

Give directions to each group and the cast.

Dramatization

Jesus with two or three disciples comes into the area where Matthew is sitting at a table collecting taxes from the people. Several people are waiting to pay their taxes. They are talking. Jesus watches. He moves up to Matthew and speaks to him.

Jesus: Matthew, I want you to come and follow me.

The crowd gets very quiet—they all look at Matthew. He thinks for a while, then he stands and says:

Matthew: OK. Where are you going?

Jesus: I'm going to your house, Matthew! It's almost dinnertime—can you feed me and my friends? It'll cost a lot of money.

Matthew: Of course—let's go.

On the way to his house, Matthew sees some of his friends. He says:

Matthew: Jesus is coming to my house. Come and have dinner with us.

The group moves with Jesus, Matthew, and the disciples and sits at a table. They begin to talk and eat. The Pharisee who is one of Matthew's friends says to one of the disciples:

Pharisee: Why is Jesus eating with tax collectors? They are not good people.

Jesus gets up and walks over to the Pharisee and says,

Jesus: Mr. Pharisee, do you ever go to the doctor?

Pharisee: Sure. Last year, I was playing and broke my leg—I had to go to the doctor and get a cast on it.

Jesus: So you go to the doctor when you're sick or hurt? Well, I'm like a doctor. I've come to help people who need my love. I am here to show mercy and kindness to all people.

Name _____

The Sower

Jesus told a story about a sower who sowed seeds. The seeds are like people who hear God's word. When you sow a seed in good soil, it grows in different stages. Read the words in the boxes. Then number the boxes from 1 to 6 to show how the seeds grow.

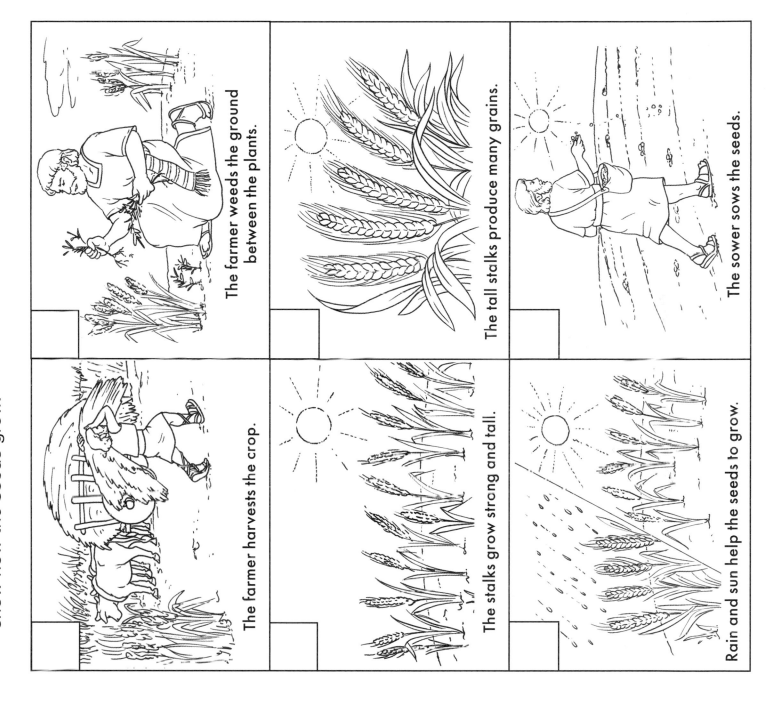

The farmer weeds the ground between the plants.

The tall stalks produce many grains.

The sower sows the seeds.

The farmer harvests the crop.

The stalks grow strong and tall.

Rain and sun help the seeds to grow.

The Sower

Based on Matthew 13:1–23

Echo Pantomime

Jesus told a story about a sower.
(Move thumb against fingers to indicate talking.)

One day the sower went out to sow seed.
(Walk in place.)

He sprinkled some of the seed onto a sidewalk.
(Hand motion of sprinkling.)

The birds came and ate the seed.
(Flap hands like birds.)

He sprinkled some of it on rocky ground.
(Hand motion of sprinkling.)

The seed started to come up but then got too dry and died.
(Wiggle hand upwards, then slowly downward.)

He sprinkled some of the seed among thorns.
(Hand motion of sprinkling.)

The thorns choked the seed.
(Make choking motion with hands.)

He sprinkled some of it on good rich soil.
(Hand motion of sprinkling.)

The seed grew up, strong and healthy.
(Hand wiggling upwards, higher and higher.)

His disciples asked Jesus, "Why did you tell this story?"
(Place fist under chin in the thinker pose.)

Jesus said, "I tell stories to help people understand my message."
(Flap thumb against fingers to indicate talking, then tap head.)

Jesus said, "Come here, I'll tell you what it means.
(Make a beckoning gesture.)

The seed sprinkled on the sidewalk is like a person who doesn't understand me.
(Hand motion of sprinkling, then hand to head while shaking head.)

The seed on the rocky ground is like someone who understands but doesn't stay with me.
(Hand motion of sprinkling, face lights up but then falls off in sleep.)

The seed on the thorns is like a person who loves other things and people more than me.
(Hand motion of sprinkling, then a motion of disgust toward the seed.)

But the seed on the good ground means a person who hears the message and understands me."
(Hand motion of sprinkling, move hands to heart.)

ACTIVITY MASTER 5

Name _____

We Prepare

Next to each picture, write down what you can do to help.

I can help by _____

I can help by _____

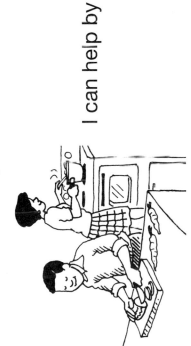

I can help by _____

I can help by _____

Washing of the Disciples' Feet

Narration

Based on John 13:1–16

Reader 1: It was just before the feast of Passover; Jesus knew that he was going to die soon. He was at a meal with his friends. He loved his friends very much. He wanted to show them how much he loved them.

Reader 2: He also wanted to give them an example of love.

ALL: Remember my love.

Reader 3: Jesus stood up from the table. He took off his cloak.

Reader 4: He took a towel and tied it around his waist.

Reader 1: Then he poured water into a large bowl and began to wash his friends' feet.

Reader 2: Where Jesus lived, the roads were very dusty. People wore sandals. When they came into a house for dinner, a servant washed their feet.

Reader 3: Jesus was not a servant, but he began to wash his friends' feet and dry them with the towel around his waist. His friends were surprised.

ALL: Remember my love.

Reader 4: Jesus came to Peter. Peter said, "Master, are you going to wash my feet?"

Reader 1: Peter could not believe what was happening. Jesus, his teacher and leader, was doing the work of a servant.

Reader 2: But Jesus said to Peter, "Right now, you do not understand what I am doing. Later, you will understand."

Reader 3: Peter was still upset. He told Jesus, "You will never wash my feet."

Reader 4: Jesus said, "Peter, if you will not let me wash your feet, you cannot be my friend." So Peter let Jesus wash his feet.

ALL: Remember my love.

Reader 1: Jesus washed everyone's feet. He put the bowl and towel away. He put on his cloak and sat down.

Reader 2: Jesus asked his friends if they understood what he had done when he washed their feet.

Reader 3: He explained to them that he wanted to give them an example of how they were to show love for each other.

Reader 4: Jesus said, "I am a servant. I am your teacher and leader but I washed your feet like a servant would. No one is greater than I am but I did the work of a servant. I want you to show your love to others by serving them like I served you. Follow my example. Be servants to each other."

ALL: Remember my love.

Name _____

Prayerful Remembrances

On the top half of this sheet, write what you are thankful for. On the bottom half, write the names of people you want to pray for.

I want to thank God for...

_____
_____
_____

I want to pray for...

_____
_____
_____

The Last Supper

Based on Matthew 26:26–28 and Luke 22:14–20

Overview

Props

- Low table
- Cushions or pillows for reclining
- Dishes and trays including a flat dish or basket for bread, dishes for vegetables and dip, and a cup for "wine"
- Unleavened bread (such as pita), grape juice, vegetables, and dip

Costume Ideas

Note: Costumes are not necessary but can add to the children's participation in and understanding of the Scriptures.

The narrator wears regular clothes. All characters may wear simple cloth or paper tunics with rope or yarn belts. All those eating should be barefoot. The servers should wear sandals and veils or turbans made from pillowcases or towels.

Setting

This dramatization may be performed in the classroom, school auditorium, or parish church.

Preparation

Familiarize yourself with the drama on page CE15. Plan how to use the space where you hold your sessions for the drama. If you are going to use them, collect props and costumes. Select children for the cast.

Cast

- Narrator
- Jesus
- Twelve Apostles or, if your group is small, select a smaller number
- Servers

Give directions to the cast. You may want to rehearse with the child selected to play the part of Jesus.

Dramatization

As the play opens, Jesus and the Apostles are seated on cushions at a low table. Servers bring trays of dishes to the table and clear away the previous course.

Narrator: On the night before he died, Jesus celebrated the Passover meal with his friends. They gathered in Jerusalem in the house of a friend. Jesus and his Apostles were talking and eating. Then Jesus got very serious.

Jesus: This is a very important night. I wanted to eat this Passover supper with you before I suffer.

Narrator: Jesus and the Apostles knew that the leaders were looking for Jesus and wanted to put him to death. This would be their last supper together. They all talked a bit more, and then Jesus asked them to be quiet.

Jesus: *(holding bread and praying)*
Blessed are you, O Lord our God, King of the Universe, who has given us this bread to eat.

Jesus breaks the bread into pieces. He passes it to the Apostles.

Jesus: Take this and eat it. This is my body which will be given for you. Do this in memory of me.

The Apostles look at one another. They eat the bread slowly and thoughtfully.

Jesus: *(picks up and holds the cup of grape juice and prays)*
Blessed are you, O Lord our God, King of the Universe, who has given us this wine to drink.

Jesus passes the cup to the Apostles and motions them to drink from it.

Jesus: Take this and drink it. This is my blood. It is the blood of a new promise God makes with you. My blood will be poured out so that the sins of many people will be forgiven.

*The servers come in to clear the table. Everyone sings. (Use Te Alabaré, Señor from the **Songs of Celebration** CD, track 12, or another familiar hymn.)*

HAND MOTIONS 7

Refrain: We come to the table of the Lord

1–2 3–4 5–6

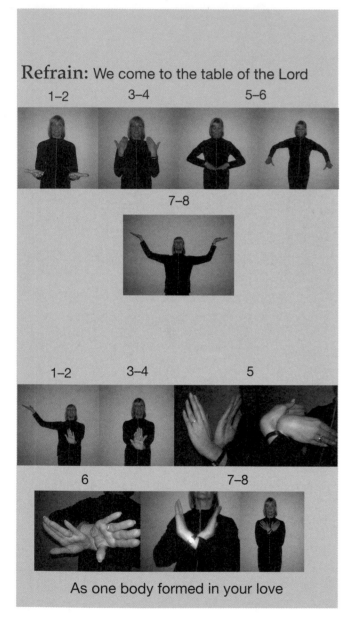

7–8

1–2 3–4 5

6 7–8

As one body formed in your love

Verse 1

1–2 3–4 5–6

7–8

Bread broken and shared to nourish us

1–2–3–4 5–6–7–8

At the table of the Lord

We come to the table of the Lord

Verse 2

1–2 3–4 5–6 7–8

Cup poured out so we will never thirst

We come to the table of the Lord

Verse 3

1–2 3–4

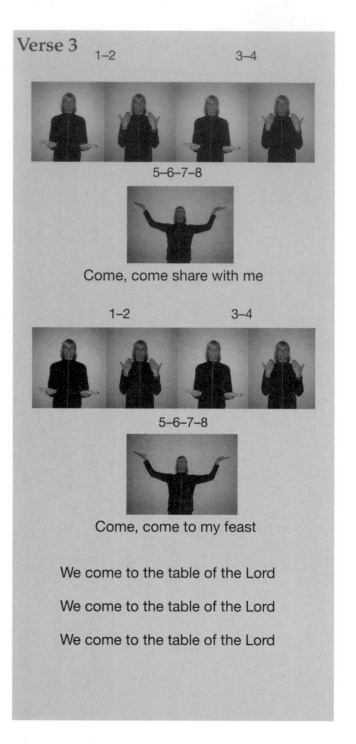

5–6–7–8

Come, come share with me

1–2 3–4

5–6–7–8

Come, come to my feast

We come to the table of the Lord

We come to the table of the Lord

We come to the table of the Lord

ACTIVITY MASTER 7

Name _____

Receiving Communion

Here are all of the steps for receiving Holy Communion. Cut them out, and then glue them in the correct order on another sheet of paper.

Answer "Amen" to "The Blood of Christ."

Say a prayer of thanksgiving.

Answer "Amen" to "The Body of Christ."

Bow before you receive the Cup.

Pray the Lamb of God.

Bow before you receive the Host.

Walk in procession to the altar.

Return to your place.

Hold your hands open or open your mouth to receive the Host.

REPRODUCIBLE

The Bread of Life

Based on John 6:32–58

Narration

Reader 1: Crowds of people followed Jesus everywhere. They listened to his stories and teachings. They saw him heal people and do other wonderful things. They came to believe he was the Messiah.

Reader 2: One day Jesus fed a large crowd of people with only five barley loaves and two fish. The people thought this was awesome. The next day they went looking for Jesus and he was gone.

Reader 3: They found Jesus in another town. They wondered when he got there. So they asked him, "Teacher, when did you get here?"

Reader 4: Jesus did not answer the question. He said, "You are looking for me because yesterday you were hungry. You ate the loaves I gave you and then you were filled. You did not see that what I did was a sign from God about who I am."

Reader 1: Jesus wanted the people to believe in him. He wanted them to do the work of God.

Reader 2: The people listened carefully to Jesus. Then they asked him, "How can we do God's work?"

Reader 3: Jesus said, "The work of God is that you believe in me, the one whom God has sent."

Reader 4: The people were not sure that God had sent Jesus. They asked Jesus for a sign. They remembered that long ago God had sent their ancestors a sign. When their ancestors were hungry in the desert God gave them bread from heaven.

NARRATION
(Continued)

Narration

Reader 1: Jesus said, "My Father gives you true bread from heaven. The bread of God comes down from heaven and gives life to the world."

Reader 2: The crowd wanted this kind of bread. They said, "Sir, give us this bread always."

Reader 3: Then Jesus said a very important thing.

Reader 4: He said, "I am the Bread of Life. Whoever comes to me will never be hungry and whoever believes in me will never be thirsty. I came down from heaven to do the Father's will. Although you have seen me, you do not believe."

Reader 1: The people were still not sure if they should believe him.

Reader 2: Some of them said, "We know Mary, his mother, and Joseph, his father. How can he say, 'I came down from heavens?'"

Reader 3: Jesus heard what they were saying. He said, "Stop talking to each other and listen to me." He wanted the people to understand that he was the Bread of Life.

Reader 4: He wanted the people to understand that everyone who believed in him would live forever.

Reader 1: Jesus told them again, "I am the bread from heaven. The people who ate manna in the desert died, as all humans die. But if you share my own flesh and blood, I will always be with you. You will live forever with God."

Reader 2: "What is he talking about?" some people asked.

Reader 3: Jesus answered them, "Whoever shares in my life will live forever. Just as the Father sent me and I have life because of him, so too will the one who eats the Bread of Life have life."

Name _____

Receiving Communion

Match the person or people with the description. Then color the pictures of the people.

Priest:
- Can celebrate Mass.
- Consecrates bread and wine into Jesus' body and blood.
- Distributes Communion.

Deacon:
- Helps priest during Mass.
- May read the Gospel and distribute Holy Communion.
- May dismiss us from Mass.

Extraordinary Ministers:
- Help priests and deacons distribute Holy Communion.

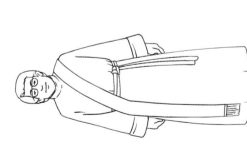

Pentecost

Based on Acts 2:1–41

Overview

Props

Desk or table and chairs
Play money on desk or table
Sign for *Peter*

Costume Ideas

Note: Costumes are not necessary but can add to the children's participation in and understanding of the Scriptures.

All characters may wear simple cloth or paper tunics with rope or yarn belts. Some may wear bathrobes as outerwear. Veils for women and headdresses for men may be improvised from pillowcases and towels. Performers may wear sandals or be barefoot.

Setting

Designate two different spaces in your session room, one for the scene in the upper room and one for the street scene. If your space is limited, do the drama in two separate scenes in a place where all can see.

Preparation

Familiarize yourself with the drama on page CE22. Plan how to use the space where you hold your sessions for the drama. If you are going to use them, collect props and costumes. Select children for the cast.

Cast

Organize the class into two groups:

• Group 1 will form the scene in the upper room.
• Group 2 will form the scene in the streets.
• 2 narrators
• Peter

Give directions to each group and the cast. Remind the children who are the disciples and the children who are the crowd that they do not speak aloud. If necessary, go over the speaking parts with the children who are playing the parts of the narrators and Peter.

DRAMA
(Continued)

Dramatization

The disciples are sitting around the table or standing in groups. Some are talking. Some are praying. The crowd is outside talking and having a good time.

Narrator 1: Not long after Jesus rose from the dead and went back to his Father, the Jewish people celebrated the feast of Pentecost. Many people came to Jerusalem for the feast.

Narrator 2: Jesus' friends were together in a house for the celebration. All of a sudden, they heard a noise like a very strong wind.

All the children make a sound like wind.

Narrator 1: They looked and saw a flame over each person's head.

All the children in the "house" look around and up over the heads of the other children and point.

Narrator 2: Each of them was filled with the Holy Spirit and began to speak in different languages. They were so excited. They jumped up and began talking very loudly about Jesus. People outside heard them and ran close to listen.

All the children in the street scene turn to the house and listen, placing their hands behind their ears.

Narrator 1: The people outside were from all over the world and they spoke different languages. But each of them understood what Jesus' disciples were saying. They asked, "What is going on?" They were amazed.

Peter moves from the house scene to the street scene.

Peter: You who are Israelites hear these words. Jesus of Nazareth was a man sent by God. God worked through him. He was crucified and died but God raised him from the dead. He received the gifts of the Holy Spirit and he sends those gifts to us now. He is Lord and Messiah, this Jesus whom you crucified.

Narrator 2: The people were very ashamed. They asked Peter, "What should we do now?"

Peter: Change your lives and be baptized.

Narrator 1: Many people who heard Peter believed in Jesus. Three thousand people were baptized that very day.

The people in the crowd come forward to Peter and say, "I believe."

Rite of Confirmation

"Those who have been baptized continue on the path of Christian Initiation through the Sacrament of Confirmation. In this Sacrament, they receive the Holy Spirit whom the Lord sent upon the Apostles on Pentecost." (1)

Catechism Connection

To deepen your own background and reflection on the Sacrament of Confirmation, refer to the *Catechism of the Catholic Church, 1830–1831.*

Catechist Resources

 The Baby in Solomon's Court
Rev. Paul Turner
Paulist Press
An introduction to the history and practice of Confirmation

 Confirmed as Children, Affirmed as Teens
James A. Wilde Ed.
Liturgy Training Publications
A collection of articles on the question of Confirmation

Children's Resources

 Who Is the Spirit? *(14 min)*
Gaynell Cronin
St. Anthony Messenger Press
Shows the Holy Spirit as friend, helper, and teacher

 God Speaks to Us in Water Stories*
Mary Ann Getty-Sullivan, Marygrace Dulski–Antkowski
Liturgical Press
Shows how God speaks to us through our world, through our history and our literature, and through other people, in our own hearts and lives

 Available at **www.harcourtreligion.com**

Catechist Formation

> "The Spirit of the Lord is upon me..."
>
> Luke 4:18

The Gift of the Holy Spirit

There are some gifts that do keep on giving. There is the large wrapped box with all kinds of little wrapped boxes inside of it. There is the first gift of flowers or fruit which is followed up every month with a new offering. There is that special gift which brings joy and happy memories each time we look at it. There is the gift which holds a promise for the future, such as, "I will care for your children for four hours on Saturday." We greet these gifts with joy and gratitude and we remember them for a long time.

While it is trite to say the gift of the Holy Spirit is a "gift that keeps on giving," the phrase may help us probe the marvel of God's gift to us. The Holy Spirit is our advocate, one who believes in us and speaks for us—always. He is our sanctifier and makes us holy. He helps us in our weakness and teaches us to pray. From the moment of our Baptism, the Holy Spirit comes to dwell in us. We become temples of the Holy Spirit, and the gift of God's love is poured out in us.

The Sacrament of Confirmation

Confirmation connects us more closely with the Church and gives us a special strength of the Holy Spirit. We receive the fullness of the Holy Spirit in the outpouring of his gifts of Wisdom, Understanding, Right Judgment or Counsel, Courage or Fortitude, Knowledge, Reverence or Piety, and Wonder and Awe or Fear of the Lord. These gifts enable us to build up the Body of Christ.

How would you describe your relationship with the Holy Spirit?

Which gift of the Holy Spirit do you use most often?

Catechist Prayer

Holy Spirit, giver of life and goodness, fill me with your divine love that I may share it with others. Amen.

Restored Order (Confirmation) **"Gifts of the Spirit" Lesson Outline**

www.harcourtreligion.com
Visit our Web site for additional resources and information.

CELEBRATE

REPRODUCIBLE

CE25

REPRODUCIBLE REPRODUCIBLE

CE26–27

OBJECTIVE:

▶ To experience the celebration of the word, including a Blessing

▶ To explain that God gives us the gift of his Holy Spirit

LESSON PROCESS:

Begin the prayer service by leading children in the Sign of the Cross. (You may want to choose a song from the *Songs of Celebration* CD as background music.) Follow the order of prayer on pages CE25–26.

▶ Help children reflect on the celebration. Ask children: What did you see? What did you hear? What did you do?

▶ Read aloud and discuss the text for the Signs of Faith on page CE26.

▶ Have children complete the activity on page CE26.

▶ Encourage children to complete the Faith at Home activity on page CE26.

▶ Summarize the text on page CE27.

▶ Read aloud the text for the Signs of Faith on page CE27.

REMEMBER

REPRODUCIBLE

CE28

OBJECTIVE:

▶ To proclaim Jesus' words about the Holy Spirit

LESSON PROCESS:

Gather children in the prayer space, and read aloud the Gospel story.

▶ Discuss children's responses to the questions.

▶ Allow time for children to complete their drawings.

REPRODUCIBLE REPRODUCIBLE

CE29   **CE30**

OBJECTIVE:

▶ To teach the meaning of the gifts of the Holy Spirit

▶ To describe part of the Rite of Confirmation

LESSON PROCESS:

▶ Read aloud the opening paragraph.

▶ Discuss each of the Gifts of the Holy Spirit.

▶ Use the Activity Master on page CE33.

▶ Read aloud the prayer of the Rite on page CE30.

▶ Encourage children to complete the Faith at Home activity on page CE30.

LIVE

REPRODUCIBLE

CE31

OBJECTIVE:

▶ To encourage children to express their desire for the gifts of the Holy Spirit

LESSON PROCESS:

Explain the activity, and have children complete it.

▶ Gather children in the prayer circle.

▶ Pray the Closing Blessing.

FAITH AT HOME

REPRODUCIBLE

CE32

OBJECTIVE:

▶ To introduce different parts of the Faith at Home page

LESSON PROCESS:

Review the five parts of the Faith at Home page with children.

▶ Encourage children to share this page with their family members at home.

Materials:

PROGRAM RESOURCES
Songs of Celebration CD

OTHER MATERIALS
Bible, cross or crucifix, prayer table, candle, large bowl filled with water

Before You Begin:

Make copies of pages CE25–CE33 for each child, and a reference copy for yourself.

Familiarize yourself with the movements of the ritual on pages CE25–26.

We Gather

Procession

As you sing, walk forward slowly. Follow the people carrying the Bible.

🎼 Sing together.

Come Lord Jesus, send us your Spirit,
renew the face of the earth.

We Are Called, David Haas © GIA Publications

Leader: God, our Father, we belong to you. We are your children. Open our hearts to the gift of the Holy Spirit. We ask this through Jesus Christ our Lord.

All: Amen.

We Listen

Leader: A reading from the holy Gospel according to John.

All: Glory to you, Lord.

Leader: Read John 14:15–26.

The Gospel of the Lord.

All: Praise to you, Lord Jesus Christ.

Sit silently.

Ritual Focus: Blessing

Leader: In Baptism you were given the gift of the Holy Spirit. By water and the Holy Spirit you received the gifts of faith and new life. Let us remember that the Holy Spirit is with us always.

Come forward one by one.

Leader: Extend your hands over the head of each child.

[Name], remember that the Holy Spirit is with you always.

Child: Amen.

We Go Forth

Leader: Loving Father, we thank you for the gift of your Spirit. Send us forth to bring your love to others. We ask this through Jesus Christ our Lord.

All: Amen.

 Sing the opening song together.

The Holy Spirit

Reflect

Power of the Holy Spirit Write a rhyme about the gift of the Holy Spirit.

The Holy Spirit lives in me.
The Holy Spirit helps me be

_____

_____

SIGNS OF FAITH

Extending Hands

One of the signs the Church uses to call upon the power of the Holy Spirit is extending hands. The priest extends his hands during the Eucharist and calls on the power of the Holy Spirit to change bread and wine into the Body and Blood of Jesus. When people are sick the priest extends his hands over them and prays that they will be healed by the power of the Holy Spirit. During the Sacrament of Confirmation, the bishop and the priests who are with him extend their hands over the people being confirmed. The bishop prays that God the Father will send the Holy Spirit upon them.

The Gift of the Holy Spirit

God gives us many gifts. He gives us the gift of creation, the gift of his Son Jesus, and the gift of the Holy Spirit. The Holy Spirit is the third Person of the Holy Trinity. The Trinity is the Church's name for the three Persons in one God.

We receive the gift of the Holy Spirit when we are baptized. He comes to live in our hearts. We cannot see the Holy Spirit, but we can see what he does. He guides the Church. He makes us holy. He is our helper.

Confirmation increases the gifts of the Holy Spirit in us. The gifts of the Holy Spirit at Confirmation help us become stronger followers of Jesus. They help us act as Jesus' disciples and share the good news about Jesus with others.

SIGNS OF FAITH

Chrism

Chrism (cri-zhum) is a mixture of olive oil and balsam. It is blessed by the bishop at a special Mass just before Easter. It is used to anoint people who are celebrating Baptism. During Baptism, chrism is put on the head of the person being baptized. During Confirmation, the bishop or priest anoints the forehead of the person receiving Confirmation. In Holy Orders the hands of the priest are anointed by the Bishop. Chrism is also used to bless new churches, chalices, patens, altars, and altar-stones, and in the solemn blessing of bells and baptismal water. The anointing with chrism is a sign of God's grace and presence.

Jesus Promises the Holy Spirit

Faith Focus

What does Jesus tell us about the Holy Spirit?

Jesus wanted his disciples to keep on sharing the good news with others even after his death and Resurrection. He knew they would need a helper.

Scripture

JOHN 14:15–17, 26, 27

During the Last Supper Jesus said to his disciples: "If you love me, you will keep my commandments. And I will ask the Father, and he will give you another Advocate, to be with you forever. You know him, because he abides with you and he will be in you….

"But the Advocate, the Holy Spirit whom the Father will send in my name, will teach you everything, and remind you of all that I have said to you. Peace I leave with you; my peace I give to you."

BASED ON JOHN 14:15–17, 26, 27

❓ **Why did the disciples need a helper?**

❓ **How can the Holy Spirit help you?**

Share

Draw a picture On a separate sheet of paper, draw a picture of one way you want the Holy Spirit to help you.

© Harcourt Religion

Faith at Home

Read the scripture story with your child. Talk about ways that the Holy Spirit helps you. Discuss times and circumstances when your child might pray to the Holy Spirit. Together pray the Come, Holy Spirit prayer on page 105 of your child's text.

REPRODUCIBLE

The Gifts of the Holy Spirit

Faith Focus

What gifts of the Holy Spirit are given at Confirmation?

The Holy Spirit is our helper too. Another name for the Holy Spirit is Advocate. *Advocate* means "helper." An advocate is someone who believes in us and supports us. The Holy Spirit is always with us to help us live as Jesus' followers.

At Confirmation, the Holy Spirit gives us seven special gifts.

Bishop

Bishops are ordained men who work with the pope in teaching and guiding the Church. They are successors of the Apostles. They teach, they help us become holy, and they show us how to tell the good news to others. Before a man is made a bishop, he is a priest. The bishop usually presides at Confirmation. Sometimes he chooses another priest to act in his place.

Wisdom helps us place God first in our life so we can make wise choices.

Understanding helps us know what our faith and life mean in God's plan.

Right Judgment or Counsel helps us make right choices and helps others to do the same.

Courage or Fortitude helps us be strong and to do what is right and avoid what is wrong.

Knowledge helps us know God and the teachings of the Church.

Reverence or Piety helps us worship and give praise to God.

Wonder and Awe or Fear of the Lord helps us know God's power and to trust him.

Confirmation

At Confirmation, the bishop talks to us. He speaks about the first Pentecost. At the first Pentecost, the Holy Spirit came to the disciples just as Jesus promised.

The bishop reminds us that we first received the Holy Spirit at Baptism. He tells us that we are to live in a way that others will see God's goodness in us. In his own words, he says:

"Christ gives different gifts to you. These gifts are given so you can build up the Body of Christ in oneness and love. Be active members of the Church, alive in Jesus Christ. With the help of the Holy Spirit, help others as Jesus did."

BASED ON RITE OF CONFIRMATION, 22

After we renew our baptismal promises, the bishop and priests extend their hands over us. The bishop sings or says this prayer,

"All-powerful God, Father of our Lord Jesus Christ,

by water and the Holy Spirit

you freed your sons and daughters from sin

and gave them new life.

Send your Holy Spirit upon them

to be their Helper and Guide.

Give them the spirit of wisdom and understanding,

the spirit of right judgment and courage,

the spirit of knowledge and reverence.

Fill them with the spirit and wonder and awe in your presence."

RITE OF CONFIRMATION, 25

© Harcourt Religion

Faith at Home

Discuss the seven gifts of the Holy Spirit with your child. Give examples of how we express these gifts in our lives. For example, when we make good choices we use wisdom and right judgment, or when we take time to admire nature or to thank and praise God we use wonder and awe. Talk about which gift you or your child needs the most.

The Holy Spirit Is with Us

Respond

Write a letter to the Holy Spirit   In the space below, write a letter to the Holy Spirit. Tell the Holy Spirit which of his gifts you most want to receive. Tell the Holy Spirit how it will help you show God's love to others.

_____

_____

_____

_____

Closing Blessing

Gather and begin with the Sign of the Cross.

Leader: God, our Father, we praise and thank you for the gift of the Holy Spirit.

All: Amen.

Leader: Jesus, our Savior, we praise and thank you for showing us how to live and love.

All: Amen.

Leader: Holy Spirit, giver of God's gifts, we praise and thank you for being our helper and guide.

All: Amen.

 Sing together.

Come Lord Jesus, send us
    your Spirit,
renew the face of the earth.

We Are Called, David Haas © GIA Publications

LIVE

Faith at Home

Faith Focus

- The Holy Spirit is the third Person of the Holy Trinity.

- The Holy Spirit is our Advocate, our helper.

- We receive the seven gifts of the Holy Spirit at Confirmation.

Ritual Focus

Blessing The celebration focused on a Blessing with the extension of hands. The children were blessed and prayed over by the catechist. During the week, use the text on page CE25 and bless your child as his or her day begins.

Act

Share Together Read the Pentecost story (Acts 2:1–12), and talk about the signs of the Holy Spirit in the reading. Use concrete and positive examples of how wind and fire affect us in our daily lives. For instance, wind creates a breeze on a hot day; fire keeps us warm. Relate the discussion to what the Holy Spirit does for us in our lives. Talk about how his coming changed the disciples. Have individual members share what they would like to receive from the Holy Spirit. Pray the Come, Holy Spirit prayer on page 105 together.

Do Together Write the names of family members on a large sheet of paper. Have family members think about what talents or gifts each member has and write them next to their names on the paper. Decide how family members together can use their gifts or talents to be of service to another family member or neighbor.

Family Prayer

Spirit of the Living God, be our helper and guide. Give us the gifts we need to live as your children and to serve one another. Amen.

Name _____

Gifts of the Holy Spirit

In the space below, write one way the Holy Spirit will be your helper. Color the gift boxes.

Wisdom

Understanding

Right Judgment or Counsel

Reverence or Piety

Wonder and Awe or Fear of the Lord

Courage or Fortitude

Knowledge

Rite of Confirmation

"This giving of the Holy Spirit conforms believers more fully to Christ and strengthens them so that they may bear witness to Christ for the building up of his Body in faith and love...." (2)

Catechism Connection

To deepen your own background and reflection on the effects of the Sacrament of Confirmation, refer to the *Catechism of the Catholic Church*, 1302–1305.

Catechist Resources

 The Church Speaks about Sacraments with Children
Mark Searle, commentator
Liturgical Press
A collection of liturgical and catechetical documents that give insight into the meaning of the sacraments

 Rethinking the Sacraments*
Bill Huebsch
Twenty Third Publications
Relates the meaning of sacraments to a contemporary spirituality

Children's Resources

 Moving On: Responding in the Spirit *(20 min)*
St. Anthony Messenger Press
A family story of moving and being challenged to follow Christ's call

 The Wondrous Adventures of Saint Francis of Assisi
Tricia Gray
St. Anthony Messenger Press
Stories of Saint Francis to help children understand holiness

 * *Available at* **www.harcourtreligion.com**

Catechist Formation

> "Who saved us and called us with a holy calling...
> Guard the good treasure entrusted to you, with the help
> of the Holy Spirit living in us."
>
> 2 Timothy 1:9,14

Called to be Holy

When we are called upon to name a holy person, we often think of people who have performed great deeds for God. Mother Teresa, Francis of Assisi, Elizabeth Seton, or Vincent de Paul would all be candidates. In them we see people of prayer and action who have done extraordinary things to build up the Body of Christ. Few of us would think of ourselves in reference to the term "holy." Some of our reluctance to include ourselves in the cast of holy ones may be that we see too much of our unholy side or it may be that for us holiness is reserved for those who do unusual things. Or "being holy" may conjure up a notion of being odd. Whatever the reason that we find ourselves reluctant to be called holy, it is not a good enough reason.

At Baptism we become part of the Body of Christ—members of "a chosen race, a holy nation, God's own people" (1 Peter 2:9). The Holy Spirit comes to dwell in us. On the one hand, we *are* holy. On the other hand, we *become* holy through the power of the Holy Spirit, who acts to make us holy and to guide us to right choices. During the Sacrament of Confirmation, prayers are said that God the Father will pour out his Holy Spirit so that we may be more like Christ and that we will give witness to Christ by our lives.

Living Witnesses

The essence of holiness is being close to God. Through the anointing at Confirmation we are sanctified or set apart to be living examples of what it means to be holy. We become holy as we deepen our relationship with God in prayer and as we continue to follow the promptings of the Holy Spirit. As we do these things, the sick are healed, the prisoners are freed, and the poor are taken care of. Through us others come to know that the kingdom of God is here.

What does the call to holiness mean for you at this point in your life?

Who are the "living witnesses" who are an example for you today?

Catechist Prayer

Holy Spirit, live in me that I may be a living witness of God's love and mercy to all those with whom I come in contact. Amen.

Restored Order (Confirmation)

"We Are Holy" Lesson Outline

www.harcourtreligion.com
Visit our Web site for additional resources and information.

CELEBRATE

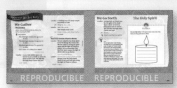

CE36–37

CE38

OBJECTIVE:
▶ To experience the celebration of the word, including the Extension of Hands in Blessing
▶ To explain that we are called to bring the light of Christ to others

LESSON PROCESS:
Begin the prayer service by leading children in a procession. (You may want to choose a song from the *Songs of Celebration* CD as background music.) Follow the order of prayer on pages CE36–37.
▶ Help children reflect on the celebration. Ask: What did you see? What did you hear? What did you do?
▶ Have children complete the activity on page CE37.
▶ Read aloud and discuss the text for the Signs of Faith on page CE37.
▶ Summarize the text on page CE38.
▶ Read aloud and discuss the text for the Signs of Faith on page CE38.

REMEMBER

CE39

OBJECTIVE:
▶ To proclaim Jesus' words about the Holy Spirit being upon him

LESSON PROCESS:
Gather children in the prayer space and read aloud the Gospel story on page CE39.
▶ Discuss children's responses to the questions.
▶ Allow time for children to complete their scrolls.
▶ Encourage children to complete the Faith at Home activity.

CE40–41

OBJECTIVE:
▶ To teach the meaning of holiness
▶ To describe parts of the Rite of Confirmation

LESSON PROCESS:
▶ Discuss the meaning of the words *holy* and *sanctified*.
▶ Explain the role of the Holy Spirit.
▶ Read aloud and discuss the Signs of Faith.
▶ Use the Activity Master on page CE44.

LIVE

CE42

OBJECTIVE:
▶ To encourage children to express how they will be living witnesses of Jesus

LESSON PROCESS:
Explain the activity and have children complete it.
▶ Gather the children in the prayer circle.
▶ Pray the Closing Blessing.

FAITH AT HOME

CE43

OBJECTIVE:
▶ To introduce different parts of the Faith at Home page

LESSON PROCESS:
Review the Faith at Home page.
▶ Encourage children to share this page at home.

Materials:

PROGRAM RESOURCES
Songs of Celebration CD

OTHER MATERIALS
Bible, cross or crucifix, prayer table, candle, large bowl filled with water

Before You Begin:

Make copies of pages CE36–44 for each child, and a reference copy for yourself.

Familiarize yourself with the movements of the ritual on pages CE36–37.

CELEBRATE

We Gather

Procession

As you sing, walk forward slowly. Follow the person carrying the Bible.

 Sing together.

We are marching in the light of God,
We are marching in the light of God.
We are marching, we are marching
   in the light of God.
We are marching, we are marching
   in the light of God.

South African Traditional

Leader: Come, Holy Spirit, open our hearts to you and fill us with the flame of your love. We ask this through Jesus Christ our Lord.

All: Amen.

Leader: A reading from the holy Gospel according to Luke.

All: Glory to you, Lord.

Leader: Read Luke 4:16–30.

The Gospel of the Lord.

All: Praise to you, Lord Jesus Christ.

Sit silently.

Ritual Focus: Extension of Hands in Blessing

Leader: We are called by the Holy Spirit to do the things that Jesus did. We are called to bring the good news and the light of Christ to others. Let us remember that the Holy Spirit keeps the light of Christ alive in us always.

Come forward one by one.

Leader: Extend hands over the head of each child.

[Name], may the Holy Spirit dwell in you and help you bring the light of Christ to others.

Child: Amen.

© Harcourt Religion

We Go Forth

Leader: Loving God, we thank you for the gifts of the Holy Spirit. Send us forth to bring your love to others. We ask this through Jesus Christ our Lord.

All: Amen.

🎼 Sing the opening song together.

SIGNS OF FAITH

Fire

On the night before Easter Sunday, the Easter fire is lit and blessed by the priest. He lights the Paschal candle from this fire. The Paschal candle is lit every time there is a Baptism. It is a sign of the light of Christ. It reminds us that Christians are called to keep the light of Christ burning in their hearts. When the Holy Spirit came to the Apostles on Pentecost, tongues of fire were seen over their heads. Fire is also a sign of the Holy Spirit and the warmth of his love.

The Holy Spirit

Reflect

Let your light shine In the space below make a list of the ways you bring good news to others.

The Light of Christ

When we sit around a campfire on a cool evening, we feel warm. If it is dark, the fire lights up the darkness and helps us see. Sometimes when we are very excited about something we want to do, people might say we are all fired up.

The light of Christ is within us. It warms us. It helps us see things better. With the help of God the Holy Spirit, it also fires us up to do Christ's work here on earth. Doing God's work is not always easy. Often we need the gifts of the Holy Spirit, especially wisdom and courage to help us.

When we do God's work, we bring the light of Christ to others. We show others what God is like. We are living examples or witnesses of what it means to be holy.

SIGNS OF FAITH

Miter and Crosier

The headdress that a bishop wears is called a miter (mi-tuhr). The bishop wears a miter at Confirmation. He also wears it at other special sacramental celebrations. The miter is shaped like a shield and ends in a peak. It also has two pieces of cloth attached to it. They hang down over the bishop's shoulders. He always wears a miter when he carries his staff. The bishop's staff is called a crosier (crow-zhur). The crosier is shaped like a shepherd's staff. It reminds us that the bishop is our shepherd.

© Harcourt Religion

Jesus Teaches About Holiness

Faith Focus

What does Jesus teach about holiness?

During his life on earth, Jesus showed the people what God was like. He told them how to be witnesses of holiness.

LUKE 4:16–30

Jesus went to the synagogue in Nazareth on the Sabbath day. Nazareth was the place where Jesus grew up. He stood up to read and was handed a scroll of the Prophet Isaiah. He read:

"The Spirit of the Lord is upon me, because he has anointed me to bring good news to the poor. He has sent me to proclaim release to the captives and recovery of sight to the blind, to let the oppressed go free, and to proclaim the year of the Lord's favor."

When he was finished everyone was looking at him. He said, "Today this scripture has been fulfilled in your hearing."

At first the people were amazed at him. They saw his power and goodness. But Jesus began to tell them that sometimes they did not do what God wanted them to do. The people became angry with Jesus.

BASED ON LUKE 4:16–30

? **What was Jesus telling the people about the Holy Spirit?**

? **Why do you need the Holy Spirit to be a witness of holiness?**

Share

Make a scroll With a partner make your own scroll. On the scroll draw or write two ways you show others that the Holy Spirit is in you.

Faith at Home

Read the scripture story with your child. Discuss the questions. Talk about ways that people today can be witnesses of Christ. Together pray the Come, Holy Spirit prayer on page 105 of your *Child's Book*. Choose one of the ways you have discussed and plan how your family can do that activity.

Holiness

Faith Focus

What does it mean to be holy?

The Holy Spirit is upon us too. One of the ways the Holy Spirit helps us is by making us holy. Being *holy* means "being close to God." It means choosing what he wants.

Another word for holy is sanctified. One of the names of the Holy Spirit is Sanctifier. He is an Advocate and a Sanctifier. Being *sanctified* means "to be set aside for a holy purpose."

When the bishop anoints us at Confirmation, we are sanctified by the Holy Spirit. We are set aside for a special purpose. We are meant to be living examples or witnesses of what it means to be holy. We are called to be saints.

SIGNS OF FAITH

Saint
Saints are people of faith who live a good life and bring the light of Christ into the world by their prayers and actions for others.

Sealed with the Spirit

During Confirmation, the bishop calls each person forward with his or her sponsor. A sponsor is a person who is a good example and witness of faith. The sponsor places his or her hand on the shoulder of the person being confirmed. The bishop dips his right thumb in the chrism and makes the Sign of the Cross on the forehead of the one being confirmed. He seals the person with the gifts of the Holy Spirit.

The bishop prays the final blessing. In the blessing he tells us what we need to do to be holy and living witnesses of Jesus.

- We use the gifts of the Holy Spirit.

- We live the Gospel.

- We want to do God's will.

- We tell others about Jesus.

We know the Holy Spirit will help us do these things.

Faith at Home

Ask your child what he or she thinks it means to be holy. Present some examples of people you both know who you think are living witnesses of Jesus or talk about a favorite saint. Discuss some ways that your child can be a sign of God's presence in the family and at school.

Being Holy

Respond

Write and draw Mark a ✓ next to the ways that show you are a living witness of Jesus. Then draw a picture of how you will tell others about Jesus.

_____ Share my things with others.

_____ Play with a friend when I do not want to.

_____ Get ahead of someone in line.

_____ Pray every day.

Closing Blessing

Gather and begin with the Sign of the Cross.

Leader: Holy Spirit, guide us to be living witnesses of Jesus. God, our Father, we praise and thank you for the gifts of the Holy Spirit.

All: Hear us we pray.

Leader: Holy Spirit, help us to be your holy children.

All: Hear us we pray.

Leader: Holy Spirit, giver of God's gifts, we praise and thank you for being our helper and guide.

All: Hear us we pray.

🎵 Sing together.

We are marching in the light of God,
We are marching in the light of God.
We are marching, we are marching
    in the light of God.
We are marching, we are marching
    in the light of God.

South African Traditional

Faith at Home

Faith Focus

- The gifts of the Holy Spirit help us do Christ's work.

- The Holy Spirit makes us holy.

- Being holy means being close to God and choosing what he wants.

Ritual Focus
Extension of Hands in Blessing

The celebration focused on the Extension of Hands in Blessing. The blessing reminded children that they are blessed with the presence of the Holy Spirit, who is guiding them to bring the light of Christ to others. At appropriate times during the week, have family members share ways they brought the light of Christ to others or how others brought the light of Christ to them. At the conclusion of the sharing, extend your hands over family members and say, "May the Holy Spirit dwell in you and help you bring the light of Christ to others."

Act

Share Together   Read the story of Jesus in the synagogue at Nazareth (Luke 4:16–30). Discuss the reading. Use these questions:

- When do you feel the Holy Spirit is in or near you?

- Do we know anyone who is sad or sick or poor and needs to have someone bring them a glad or happy message?

- How could we take a happy message to them?

Do Together   Discuss the idea of what it means to be a living witness. Have individual family members name people whom they think are living witnesses of faith—people who bring the light of Christ to others. Of the people mentioned, select one or two whom the whole family knows. Together decide on an appropriate way to thank the person for his or her witness. You might make a card or write a note and send it to him or her or do something anonymously that would be of service to him or her.

Family Prayer

Spirit of the Living God, live in us so we may be witnesses of Christ's light and life to others. Amen.

GO ONLINE **www.harcourtreligion.com**
Visit our Web site for weekly scripture readings and questions, family resources, and more activities.

Name _____

We Are Holy

Read the ways people are holy. In the fourth space draw a picture of one way you are holy. Color the drawings on the page.

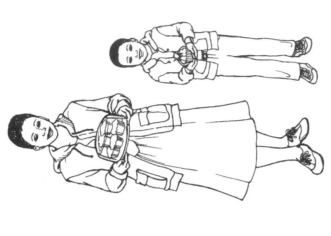

We feed the hungry.

We show care for others.

I am holy when I _____ .

We stay close to God.

CE44